Neil Joeck

Maintaining Nuclear Stability in South Asia

Adelphi Paper 312

Oxford University Press, Great Clarendon Street, Oxford OX2 6DP

Oxford New York

Athens Auckland Bangkok Bombay Calcutta Cape Town
Dar es Salaam Delhi Florence Hong Kong Istanbul Karachi
Kuala Lumpur Madras Madrid Melbourne Mexico City
Nairobi Paris Singapore Taipei Tokyo Toronto
and associated companies in
Berlin Ibadan

Oxford is a trade mark of Oxford University Press

Published in the United States
by Oxford University Press Inc., New York

First published September 1997 by **Oxford University Press** for
The International Institute for Strategic Studies
23 Tavistock Street, London WC2E 7NQ
http://www.isn.ethz.ch/iiss

British Library Cataloguing in Publication Data
Data available

Library of Congress Cataloguing in Publication Data

ISBN 0-19-829406-9
ISSN 0567-932x

contents

maps

Map I *South Asia*

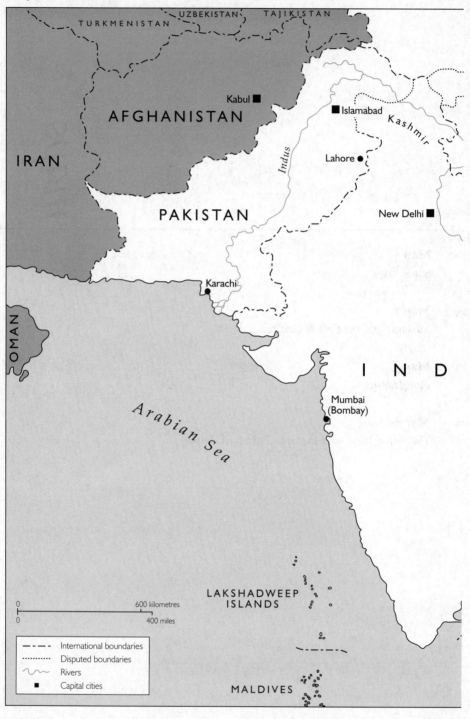

TURKMENISTAN   UZBEKISTAN   TAJIKISTAN

AFGHANISTAN

Kabul ■

IRAN

Islamabad ■

Indus

Kashmir

Lahore ●

PAKISTAN

New Delhi ■

OMAN

Karachi ●

I N D

Arabian Sea

Mumbai
(Bombay) ●

0 ————————— 600 kilometres
0 ————————— 400 miles

LAKSHADWEEP
ISLANDS

—·—·— International boundaries
·········· Disputed boundaries
～～ Rivers
■ Capital cities

MALDIVES

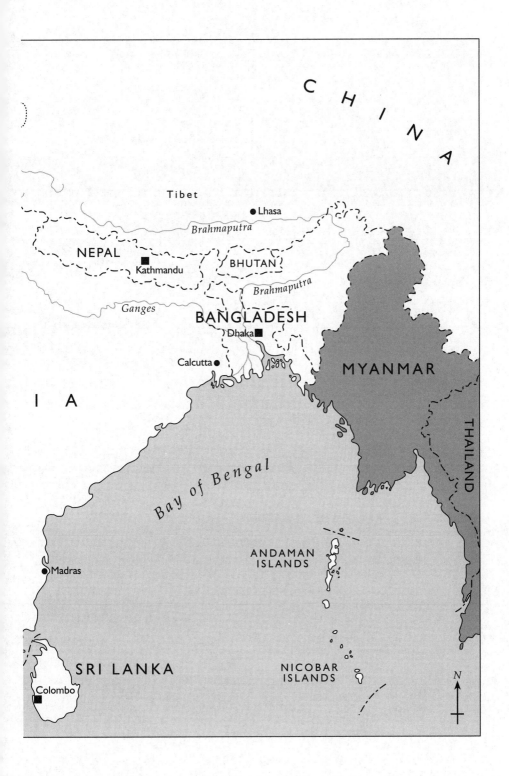

glossary

CSBM	Confidence- and Security-Building Measure
CTBT	Comprehensive Test Ban Treaty
DAE	Department of Atomic Energy (India)
DGMO	Director-General of Military Operations
FMCC	Fissile Material Cut-off Convention
GSQR	General Staff Quality Review
HEU	Highly Enriched Uranium
HUMINT	Human Intelligence
IAEA	International Atomic Energy Agency
IHE	Insensitive High Explosive
IRBM	Intermediate-Range Ballistic Missile
NPT	Nuclear Non-Proliferation Treaty
NWFP	North-west Frontier Province (Pakistan)
PAEC	Pakistan Atomic Energy Commission
PAL	Permissive Action Link
SIGINT	Signals Intelligence
SRBM	Short-Range Ballistic Missile
UNCIP	UN Commission in India and Pakistan

Fifty years after their violent formation, India and Pakistan continue to face each other across a hostile and in places heavily armed border. Their conflict is marked by limited dialogue and intractable domestic and international disputes. Nuclear weapons now shadow their relations, and both sides may soon develop and deploy ballistic missiles.[1]

Proponents of an explicit nuclear-weapon capability in South Asia argue that these conditions have made war unlikely given that both players' nuclear capabilities make a disabling first strike impossible.[2] Mutual fears of catastrophe regardless of a war's outcome are therefore thought to make another conflict between the two sides almost impossible.[3] Some nuclear proponents also feel that the existence of even a veiled nuclear capability prevented crises between the two countries in 1987 and 1990 from spilling over into war, and would also have prevented prior wars had it been in place.[4]

Nuclear proponents maintain that, because past Indo-Pakistani conflicts were limited, future wars would in any case not involve the use of nuclear weapons. The two countries' three major wars were indeed limited in the sense that civilian and battlefield casualties were light, and the last two, in 1965 and 1971, were concluded within about two weeks. Internal strife in both countries, especially in Pakistan during the civil war preceding the creation of Bangladesh, has resulted in greater loss of life.[5] Finally, many Indian analysts argue that China is the real threat anyway, and claim that

Western analysts are unnecessarily fixated on the India–Pakistan confrontation.[6]

This paper takes a less optimistic view. It begins with two assumptions. First, India and Pakistan are unlikely to reverse their nuclear programmes in the next five to ten years.[7] Both countries consider their national security to be threatened and believe that a nuclear capability is critical to the safety of the nation. Furthermore, they attained their nuclear status despite enormous outside pressure over two decades. This pressure, combined with sometimes exaggeratedly defiant internal rhetoric, has elevated the issue symbolically, making reversal politically hazardous.

The second assumption is that both sides may soon develop and deploy short-range ballistic missiles (SRBMs). Although SRBMs may not be intended as nuclear-weapon delivery vehicles, both countries might assume that they could be configured to carry such weapons. This would dramatically change both sides' ability to manage escalation and to calculate behaviour in a crisis. The short flight times of SRBMs, the inability to recall them once launched and the requirement to delegate command compound those problems.

This paper argues that India and Pakistan's nuclear capabilities have not created strategic stability, do not reduce or eliminate factors that contributed to past conflicts, and therefore neither explain the absence of war over the past decade nor why war is currently unlikely. The influence of non-state actors (Kashmiri insurgents and unofficial government representatives), domestic disturbances (for example, in East Bengal and Punjab), and shortcomings in decision-making (concentration of power in the executive branch, limited intelligence) all contribute to instability.

The view that nuclear capability creates deterrence assumes that the shadow it casts makes conflicts less likely, more manageable, or even avoidable. However, this view ignores the important strategic and tactical implications of acquiring a nuclear capability. Far from creating stability, these basic nuclear capabilities have led to an incomplete sense of where security lies. Limited nuclear capabilities increase the potential costs of conflict, but do little to reduce the risk of it breaking out. Nuclear weapons may make decision-makers in New Delhi and Islamabad more cautious, but sources of conflict immune to the nuclear threat remain.

The development of command-and-control mechanisms would enhance stability in a crisis and improve the ability to avoid nuclear use in the event of war. Operational considerations – nuclear doctrine, weapons' safety, alternative response options, intelligence and early warning – would help to reinforce deterrence at ground level and ensure that both sides are not left with a choice between suicide and surrender.

A set of diplomatic steps must also be considered. In the absence of a defence against nuclear attack, bilateral confidence- and security-building measures (CSBMs) might reduce the likelihood of war and limit its consequences should war break out. Two dangerous but important areas needing attention are missile deployment and conventional force reductions. Agreements on issues such as trade, energy, military hotlines, security pledges and fissile-material control would not compromise security, but could capitalise on the positive diplomatic relations created in early 1997. It is time to think again about ways to reduce nuclear risks.

chapter 1

Prospects for War

War between India and Pakistan is currently unlikely as conflict management appears to have replaced military action as a means of settling disputes. A May 1997 meeting in the Maldives between Indian Prime Minister Inder Gujral and his Pakistani counterpart Mohammed Nawaz Sharif was warm and open, and created a sense of common purpose in frequently bitter bilateral relations. Positive foreign-secretary-level talks the following month established working groups to discuss a range of contentious issues.[1]

Indo-Pakistani relations have, however, always been marked by ups and downs and, regardless of the personal *bonhomie* between the two prime ministers, it cannot be assumed that they will retain power or that their goodwill is shared throughout their countries. If Gujral and Sharif are unable to overcome fundamental differences despite their touted *rapprochement*, it may be difficult to avoid relapsing into bitterness and recrimination.

Overcoming historical enmities and institutionalising amicable relations will therefore remain a challenge. It is noteworthy, however, that the two countries have avoided open, cross-border conflict since 1971 – over half their history as independent nations – and have weathered potentially dangerous confrontations in 1987 and 1990.[2] Since 1989, Pakistani-backed insurgents have disrupted Kashmir, prompting Indian police and military forces to respond at times with savage repression, but war has been avoided. Troops have faced each other for over a decade across northern Kashmir's

Siachen Glacier, but again the conflict has been contained. In addition to these armed confrontations, a diplomatic freeze in January 1994–March 1997 did not increase military tensions.

Given this record of avoiding confrontation, neither side expects war to break out. Indians express confidence that they will not start a war, and that Pakistan is deterred from doing so. Pakistanis are less confident that India will not initiate conflict, but by the same token do not see themselves doing so, even over Kashmir.[3]

This confidence will not, however, prevent the re-emergence of factors that could undermine stability in the future.[4] Past conflicts and crises have been heavily influenced by inadvertent escalation, misperception and the law of unintended consequences; national decision-makers have found it difficult to control the development and pace of crises. Wars and crises might have been avoided in the past but for the intervention or influence of a number of non-rational or uncontrollable factors. A major study of nuclear proliferation in South Asia concludes:

> *Behaviour before and during the region's major wars does not inspire confidence that both sides will understand and manage the risks of escalation to nuclear war. Similarly, several retrospective studies of the crises of 1987 and 1990 show a combination of misperception, risk taking, bad intelligence, and disarray in decision-making reminiscent of US and Soviet behaviour during the Cuban missile crisis.*[5]

Although nuclear weapons impose some restraint on decision-makers in New Delhi and Islamabad, non-state actors, domestic politics and decision-making structures may be impervious to central authority and may cause conflicts in the future.

The Influence of Non-State Actors
Kashmir
The almost decade-long disruption of Kashmir has not caused war between India and Pakistan, but it remains a potential flashpoint.[6] Gujral's comment in May 1997 sums up the Indian position: 'Sovereignty of India and the secular unity of India are non-

negotiable.' Pakistan's position is equally clear: '[Kashmir is] a core issue [and] cannot be put on the backburner.'[7] Pakistan rests its case on legal, moral and ideological grounds, arguing that UN resolutions in the 1950s calling for a plebiscite must be honoured. Pakistan argues that the will of the Kashmiri people can only be expressed in a plebiscite; India claims that this will has already been voiced through democratic elections.

This stand-off is unlikely to change without significant compromise. Although Sharif enjoys a commanding electoral majority, he cannot afford to retreat from the demand for a plebiscite. Gujral and his successors are likely to remain coalition-builders rather than leaders of a majority party, making bold departures on Kashmir unlikely. Given continued rhetorical

the possibility of war cannot be ignored

confrontation and military tension, the possibility of war cannot be ignored. Past history indicates that local insurgents or separatists may take initiatives that could be difficult to control.

The first Kashmir war, in 1947–48, typifies how local activity can force the hand of central decision-makers.[8] Soon after partition in August 1947, reports of atrocities against Kashmiri Muslims prompted tribal forces in Pakistan's North-west Frontier Province (NWFP) to launch a holy war of assistance. Once the tribal forces were engaged, Pakistani Prime Minister Mohammed Ali Jinnah apparently authorised some regular troops, who had been granted home leave, to join the campaign. The Pakistani government had not provoked or encouraged the campaign, and 'refrained from helping the tribesmen primarily because of the fear of provoking a large-scale war between Pakistan and India'.[9]

Jinnah's restraint did not prevent war from breaking out. The ill-planned tribal offensive bogged down before reaching Srinagar, the capital of Kashmir. The prospect of being overrun convinced the Kashmiri Maharaja, Hari Singh, to accede to India. This decision, at a critical moment when the tribal forces were looting the cities they had captured, allowed Indian reinforcements to be airlifted to Srinagar. India mounted its own offensive six months later in April 1948, when spring made conditions more conducive for war. India's regular army was superior to the tribal forces and, fearing that India would carry its offensive into Pakistan, Jinnah escalated the conflict by committing two divisions to the battle. The war dragged on until the UN Commission on India and Pakistan (UNCIP) secured a cease-fire in August 1948. A war that neither Pakistan nor India wanted established the terms for their relations thereafter.

Although India and Pakistan fought a further war over Kashmir in 1965, the danger of local insurgency only emerged again in 1990, when terrorists almost provoked a conflict. The origins of that confrontation can be traced to then Indian Prime Minister Rajiv Gandhi's attempts to manipulate the outcome of state elections in 1987. Gandhi's efforts sparked a surge of terrorism, which resulted in the kidnap of the Indian Home Minister's daughter in late 1989. Although she was released unharmed, a war of words ensued between India's six-month-old government, headed by V. P. Singh, and Pakistan's one-year-old administration under Benazir Bhutto. Singh accused Pakistan of interfering in Indian domestic politics through its support of Kashmiri radicals, while Bhutto argued that the insurrection was spontaneous and reinforced the need to honour the UN's call for a plebiscite. Neither leader could easily back down as they each rested on shaky political ground. Singh was the leader of an unstable coalition government, while Bhutto, as Prime Minister, was subject to dismissal by Pakistan's President under the terms of the Constitution.

Heated threats were exchanged (Bhutto warned of a 1,000-year war, to which Singh countered that Pakistan might not last 1,000 hours), but both sides refrained from moving their forces into offensive positions. As tensions mounted, Pakistani Foreign Minister Sahabzada Yaqub Khan flew to New Delhi, where he held a strained meeting with his counterpart, Inder Gujral. The US was sufficiently concerned that in May it sent a high-level delegation under Deputy National Security Advisor Robert Gates to the region to mediate.

In the end, the 1990 confrontation came to little more than a war of words. It was followed by a series of lesser crises and an attempted march across the Line of Control dividing Kashmir in 1992. In February 1992, demonstrators on the Pakistani side threatened to move across the dividing line to support Kashmiris on the Indian side. The Pakistani authorities ordered their troops to confront the demonstrators, prevent the march and maintain peace.

Map 2 *Kashmir and the Line of Control*

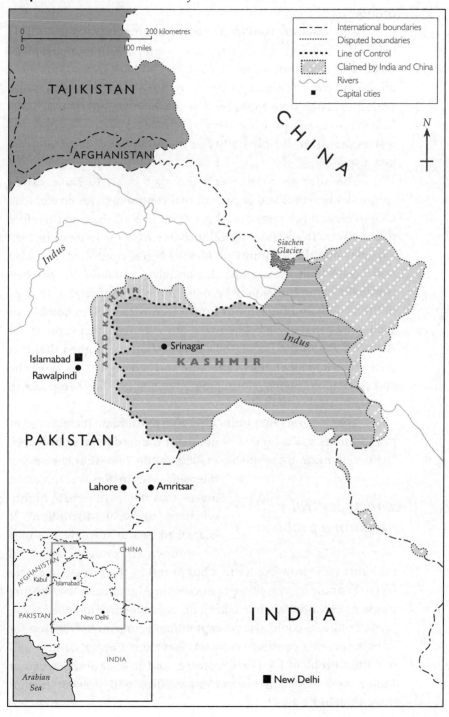

Several demonstrators were shot, and events did not get out of control.[10]

Low-intensity conflict has since continued, and there is little evidence to suggest that Pakistan is prepared to compromise. Islamabad does not support Kashmiri independence, but even incoherent conflict, although increasing tensions, alleviates pressure within Pakistan from those keen on stronger action. It also drains Indian resources – pleasing many in Islamabad. As long as the issue festers, however, the possibility of it getting out of hand must be taken seriously.

The 1947–48 conflict and the 1990 crisis to some extent contradict the confident argument that central decision-makers are able to control behaviour on the ground in Kashmir and therefore prevent war. The relative restraint shown over the issue since 1989 suggests that the Kashmiri problem is better controlled. It is also noteworthy that India and Pakistan have contained the Siachen conflict (although this may be more a function of terrain than of political will) and the fall-out from a terrorist attack in Bombay in 1994, which may have been carried out with Pakistani support. Dr Ashley Tellis of the US' RAND Corporation has argued that this restraint is largely on the Indian side and is designed to ensure the success of its economic reform programme, rather than a response to Pakistan's nuclear status.[11]

This suggests that India feels able to calibrate its response to provocations in Kashmir. The nature of the conflict may, however, change significantly, while the inability of the two sides to extricate themselves from the confrontation means that they will remain highly sensitive to local disruption. If Islamabad tries to move the Kashmir issue down its priority list, local militants may grow bolder in a bid to return their cause to centre stage. In addition, the *Taleban*'s success in Afghanistan may inspire militants in Kashmir, while *Taleban* fighters may drift into the region. *Taleban* setbacks could also prompt militants to scan the horizon for more promising causes to support elsewhere. Central control will remain a problem for years to come, and it is doubtful whether Indian and Pakistani nuclear capabilities will prevent further disruption in Kashmir.

central control will remain a problem

The *Brasstacks* Crisis

The *Brasstacks* crisis in 1987 again demonstrates the extent to which non-state actors can exacerbate Indo-Pakistani hostilities. The *Brasstacks* exercise, the most extensive set of manoeuvres in Indian history, was marked by limited information, poor communication and lax political control. The exercise was conducted dangerously close to Pakistan's south-eastern border. The field portion, held in January 1987, was especially controversial but, after a tense border stand-off, a diplomatic solution appeared imminent in the closing days of the month.

At that point, on 28 January, Dr Abdul Qadir Khan, the man responsible for Pakistan's uranium-enrichment programme, received a visit from a Pakistani journalist, Mushahid Hussain, whom he described as an old friend. Hussain was accompanied by an Indian journalist, Kuldip Nayar. A month after the visit, Nayar released what he referred to as an interview in which Khan is said to have warned that Pakistan was capable of producing nuclear weapons, and that 'we shall use the bomb if our existence is threatened'.[12] Although the 'interview' was conducted on 28 January, it was not published until 1 March. It has never been made clear whether Nayar communicated what he considered to be a nuclear threat against India to the government in New Delhi before publication.

Beyond agreement that Nayar and Hussain did indeed visit Khan, few stories about the incident correspond. According to Nayar, the interview was planned and was intended for publication. Khan, by contrast, claimed that he merely received a visit from his friend to invite him to his wedding reception; Nayar happened to accompany him. Hussain at one point claimed that the remarks were expressly intended as a message to India from Pakistani President Mohammed Zia ul-Haq. In any case, few of the principal actors in the *Brasstacks* crisis felt that the Nayar–Khan discussion influenced its outcome.

Regardless of the incident's effect on the crisis, it is clear that, as in other countries, executive control cannot extend to every person and every action. Although the Nayar meeting took place several days after the diplomatic resolution of the crisis, this may have been simply the result of late timing by Hussain in arranging the interview, either as a result of his ignorance that the crisis was being resolved, or of a desire to influence the course of the negotiations under way at the end of January. If Zia set up the meeting specifically to send a signal, it makes the issue of command and control in a crisis all the more ambiguous. The Khan interview (or non-interview) could have been interpreted by India, had it been conveyed by Nayar in a timely manner, as a threat that could not be ignored.

Whom is India to believe the next time a veiled threat is issued? In a future crisis, a key government official may make statements or take actions which are perceived by the opposing side to represent government policy. Possessing a nuclear capability does not eliminate the possibility of such provocations. Future crises may be exacerbated despite central decision-makers' efforts to maintain control. Although the risk of unofficial government actors sending – or being wrongly perceived to be sending – signals may be less of a problem than the Khan 'interview' would suggest, it nevertheless strongly argues for tight control, particularly if missiles are deployed on both sides of the border. When the fuse on a crisis is long and each side has the space and time to draw back, signals can be analysed and discussed and hasty overreactions avoided. In the absence of systematised control, a false signal may be taken as authentic, while an intentional signal may be ignored.

The Influence of Domestic Politics

The Bangladesh crisis in 1970–71 is the best historical example of a war into which India and Pakistan were drawn by domestic factors.[13] Before 1970, Pakistan had not fully integrated all parts of the state. Bengali grievances in East Pakistan worsened until elections in December. The East Pakistan-based Awami League, led by Sheikh Mujibur Rahman, won convincingly in the East but received effectively no support in West Pakistan. Conversely, Zulfiqar Ali Bhutto's Pakistan People's Party (PPP) won a decisive majority in the West, but virtually no support in the East. The Awami League, which endorsed extensive devolution of power, emerged with a nationwide majority and claimed the right to form a government. Chief Martial Law Administrator Yahya Khan, strongly influenced by Bhutto's self-interested arguments, was reluctant to

Map 3 *Bangladesh*

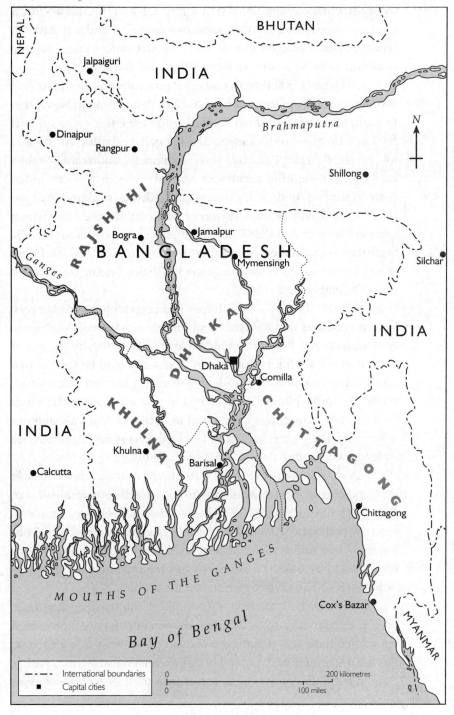

allow it to do so, prompting the aggrieved Awami League to declare the East independent. In March 1971, Yahya responded with a military crackdown. Within months, up to 10 million Muslim refugees had streamed out of East Pakistan into India, severely straining social structures in West Bengal and India.

Pakistan's inability to solve its own internal problems had become a security problem for India. New Delhi began in November to infiltrate irregular Indian soldiers into East Pakistan to support the large numbers of Indian-trained Bengali guerrillas. Aware that his forces in East Pakistan were extremely vulnerable, Yahya launched pre-emptive air attacks against bases in western India. Now equipped with a legal *casus belli*, India declared war on Pakistan and within days its forces had reached the outskirts of Dhaka, the capital of East Pakistan. Intense negotiations at the UN Security Council failed to produce a cease-fire until Indian forces closed in on Pakistan's headquarters in Dhaka, forcing a surrender on 17 December 1971.

As 1970 drew to a close, hopes had been high that democracy had worked and that Pakistan could resolve its internal problems. Neither India nor Pakistan would have predicted that, by the end of 1971, they would fight a bitter war, Pakistan would be split in two and nuclear weapons would begin to cast a shadow over future relations. India planned carefully for war soon after the crisis erupted, but would never have had to fight one had Pakistan not mismanaged its internal affairs. Domestic chaos had dramatically transformed South Asia's international politics.

Domestic political factors also played a role in the *Brasstacks* crisis, helping to escalate tensions and increase the possibility of war. Pakistan had supported Sikh radicals – then actively working for a separate homeland, Khalistan – in India even before *Brasstacks*. Once the crisis was under way, Indian fears that radicals would assist or be exploited by Pakistan prompted escalatory behaviour that may not have been called for by events on the ground.

Pakistan had initially responded cautiously as *Brasstacks* unfolded in January 1987. Based on its own intelligence, however, it feared that India was planning to convert the exercise into an attack. Pakistan was ending its own annual exercises at the time. Rather than immediately moving his forces into their peacetime cantonments, the commanding general, Khalid Mahmud Arif, deployed his armoured units north of the Sutlej River to ensure that his troops would be optimally positioned defensively if Indian troops attacked. Arif deliberately positioned his troops in such a way as to allow Indian reconnaissance to recognise their defensive posture.

To Arif's surprise, his troop movements went undetected for two weeks. When they were located by Indian intelligence, their defensive positioning went unnoticed and near-panic ensued in New Delhi as Indian officials feared that Arif was readying his troops to attack. Positioned as they were on the north of the Sutlej, the Pakistani troops could have reoriented and attacked India's vulnerable points in Punjab, with the Sutlej River as a buffer on the right flank. The Punjab border, which posed significant challenges to any attacking armour because of the extensive canal system in the area, was heavily defended during the exercise. Even so, Indian reinforcements were sent scrambling to confront Arif's forces if they moved into India.

India's alarm was explained by its fear that Pakistan might try to exploit Sikh grievances in Punjab. As Indian forces would have to move through Punjab, they would face possible rearguard action from Sikh dissident groups. The parallel with the formation of Bangladesh was obvious. Pakistan had launched pre-emptive attacks in 1971 when it saw India exploiting its domestic weakness in the East. India escalated too in 1987 when it feared that Pakistan would do the same in Punjab.

The effect of the Bengali uprising on the 1971 war and the Sikh insurrection on the 1987 crisis challenge current arguments that nuclear capabilities will help to avoid war. It was clear at the beginning of 1971 that neither side expected or wanted war, yet when Pakistan tried to solve its domestic problems by force it created an international crisis. Similarly, in 1987, although neither side wanted war, the possibility that Pakistan would exploit India's domestic problems created ripples that moved both sides close to conflict. Decisions made in New Delhi and Islamabad did not prevent a domestic dispute from becoming war in 1971, and causing a crisis – which India may have mistakenly assumed it could calibrate and manage – to escalate to the brink of war in 1987. India's nuclear capability did not prevent Pakistan from supporting Sikh

Map 4 *The Sutlej River and the Indo-Pakistani Border*

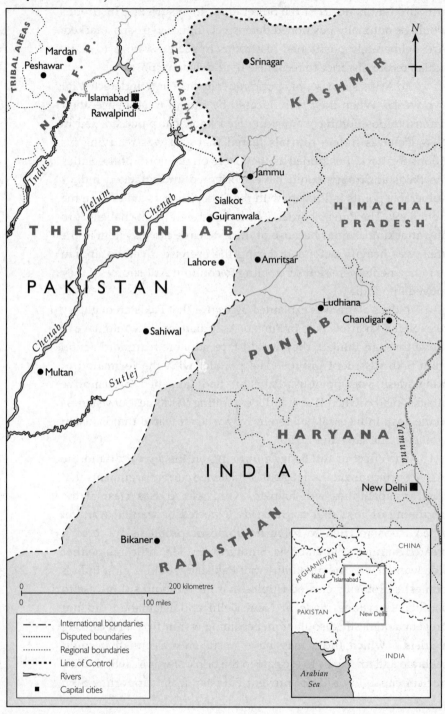

grievances in 1987, but more importantly it did not stabilise the crisis by allowing India to wait it out. Gandhi was not confident that India's nuclear capability would prevent conflict.

Given that India and Pakistan continue to face internal problems, similar crises could develop. Nuclear weapons may make decision-makers in New Delhi and Islamabad cautious, but they appear to have little effect on the national aspirations of disaffected citizens within the two countries.

How serious are the two countries' domestic problems? India has been troubled by internal dislocations throughout its history, but has shown remarkable resilience and has weathered two funda- mental challenges to its integrity. The Kashmir separatist movement may have lost some momentum, and the radical Sikh effort to create a separate state of Khalistan appears to be under control, although India continues to be plagued by sporadic

how serious are domestic problems?

terrorist activity.[14] Rebels in the north-east continue to attack military targets and isolated villages, but, although the disputes show no sign of fading away, they equally show no sign of tearing India apart. Other than Kashmir, therefore, India's internal problems are unlikely in the near term to provide Pakistan with an opportunity to intervene, nor are they likely to escalate to such an extent that war would result.[15]

Kashmir, however, remains a serious issue. Islamabad cannot let it drop, but must assiduously retain control over those it supports. New Delhi continues to assert its sovereignty, but does not push its military enforcement to the point of war. At the same time, the Kashmiris themselves are anxious to assert their own will, which may run counter to Indian and Pakistani policies alike. It is a balancing act for both sides that will be difficult to maintain, as local forces capable of pressuring both India and Pakistan will be unaffected by their nuclear capabilities.

Three areas of concern may exacerbate Pakistan's domestic problems: the Mohajir Qaumi Movement (MQM); the Sunni–Shi'a conflict; and the *Taleban*.[16] Intense repression during the last two years of Benazir Bhutto's term of office from 1995–96 significantly reduced MQM violence in its power-base, Karachi. In campaigning to defeat Bhutto in the February 1997 elections, the eventually victorious Muslim League (N) promised the MQM greater political legitimacy and involvement in Sindh and Karachi. Violence has since increased and may easily spread unless the MQM's demands are met.

At least as dangerous is a second internal division, that between the Sunni and Shi'a in the Punjab. A spate of murders and bombings in early 1997 forced the government to consider banning radical Sunni groups, but pushing the problem underground will not solve it. With Iranian 'cultural' centres one of the targets for Sunni radicals, an international dimension has emerged which worries many Pakistanis.

This issue is complicated by a third potential internal problem associated with the success of the *Taleban* movement in Afghanistan. Iran sees the *Taleban* as a product of Pakistani policy and as detrimental to its security. In combination with the attacks on Shi'a communities, Iran may respond to Pakistan's support of the *Taleban* by exploiting Pakistan's sectarian strife. At the same time, if the *jihad* in Afghanistan heads to a conclusion, troublemakers and hardened terrorists may begin to appear in Pakistan. Already tense ethnic and sectarian rivalries could become far worse with the addition of passionate believers who have little stake in Pakistan's stability.

Pakistan's internal problems may again affect India. Problems in Sindh are unlikely to leak across the border as did the Bengali grievances in 1971, and Sunni–Shi'a violence is unlikely to affect India's Muslim community. But longer-term potential problems arising from the chaos in Afghanistan could seriously hamper New Delhi's ability to control events in Kashmir. Although many Indians argue that the country is able to restrain its actions in Kashmir, that violence there is dissipating and that low-intensity conflict will not escalate into crisis, the combination of variables in Pakistan's domestic scene could cause things to go awry. The experiences of 1971 and 1987 suggest that Indian and Pakistani nuclear capabilities may have little influence on future crises springing from domestic factors.

The Influence of Decision-Making

Several factors have compromised rational decision-making in past Indo-Pakistani conflicts. These factors include high-risk war planning motivated by biased analysis, assumptions about the influence of outside actors, stress, excessive centralisation and intelligence failures. In this respect, India and Pakistan are no different from many other nations caught up in rivalry and enmity. These factors alone may not cause war to break out, but, taken together, they undermine confidence in decision-makers' ability to manage crises and avoid conflict.

Knowing that a nuclear war cannot be won, neither India nor Pakistan is likely to conduct a premeditated attack.[17] It is worth noting, however, that high-risk decisions to start wars have been made in the past despite strong indications that the war would be lost, and even when the other side had nuclear weapons. In 1941, Japan decided to initiate conflict with the US in the erroneous belief that Washington would be willing to fight only a limited war. In 1973, Egypt decided to attack Israel in the full knowledge that it could not win a protracted conflict, but in the belief that outside actors would intervene to stop the war before that stage was reached. Furthermore, President Anwar Sadat was prepared to take the gamble despite Israel's possible possession of nuclear weapons. In 1981, Argentina, disregarding the UK's nuclear weapons, seized the Falkland Islands, apparently believing that London would respond through negotiation rather than war. The rout of Argentina's forces put paid to such delusions and marked the end of military rule in Buenos Aires.

Similar high-risk decisions have been taken in South Asia. In 1965, Pakistan's Ayub Khan launched a war in Kashmir even though evidence indicated that he could not win a protracted conflict. Expectations that Kashmir would rise up against India and that New Delhi would confine its response to the Kashmir front were mistaken, but military operations went ahead nonetheless.[18] Pakistan's leaders (Khan and then Foreign Minister Zulfiqar Ali Bhutto) refused to accept or to act upon information that contradicted their beliefs, based in part on a misinterpretation of India's 'passive' response to an earlier dispute. This biased thinking may no longer characterise Pakistani planning, but the larger point is that biases continue to influence decision-making.

A particularly troubling belief embraced almost unquestioningly by Pakistanis is that India is bent on subduing or even demolishing their country. This belief has been reinforced by the break-up of Pakistan in 1971, by occasional comments by right-wing Indian politicians that the 1947 partition of India was a mistake, and by Pakistani intelligence which, in 1987, indicated that India planned an attack. This fatalism may make decision-makers in Islamabad more resigned to using nuclear weapons in extreme circumstances. It could be dangerous, therefore, to assume that war is unlikely simply because rational calculations during peacetime indicate that starting a war would lead to catastrophe. Although both sides may correctly assess the other as being reluctant to begin a war, it is easy to miscalculate the outcome of events and then find it difficult to reimpose control.

The expectation that outside players would intervene to stop conflict has also influenced South Asian decision-making. The UN played an active role in resolving the 1947–48 war by helping to negotiate a cease-fire. In 1965, the Soviet Union stepped in to mediate a formal end to that conflict and, in 1990, early intervention by the US may have prevented escalation.[19] Timely external intervention is, however, by no means guaranteed: in 1962, the US responded to Prime Minister Jawaharlal Nehru's request for help too late to prevent India's humiliation at the hands of China. Similarly, Yahya Khan hoped in vain for last-minute US intervention to avert defeat by India in 1971. The magnitude of a war which could include the use of nuclear weapons may make third parties more inclined to intervene in a future crisis – but may equally increase their reluctance to become involved. In either case, the historical record should discourage both sides from assuming that third parties will necessarily be able to provide timely intervention to prevent or limit another war.

crises can lead to escapist thinking

The element of stress should also give pause to confident assessments that war will be avoided in South Asia. Rational decision-makers, knowing that they face nuclear retaliation, may not plan an attack. However, crises can lead to escapist thinking and human failings may overwhelm good judgement. For example, Khan's belief in the closing days of the 1971 war that the US might somehow rescue East Pakistan may have been inspired more by excessive drinking than by rational calculations.[20] When the effect of stress on decision-making is considered in the light of Pakistan's history of striking first, as in 1965 and 1971, rather than allowing the battle to be brought to its own territory, it should not be assumed that India and Pakistan's limited nuclear capabilities will necessarily prevent future conflict.

Excessively centralised decision-making also poses potential problems. The *Brasstacks* exercise, for example, was planned by a small circle of officials who apparently did not carefully consider how Pakistan would respond to such a massive show of force. This restricted decision-making was followed by Prime Minister Rajiv Gandhi's exclusion from the loop when the issue reached crisis proportions.

Gandhi was holidaying in the Andaman Islands as the crisis loomed in January 1987. In his absence, *Brasstacks* was managed by Minister of State for Defence Arun Singh and the Chief of Army, General K. S. Sundarji. They decided not to alert Gandhi until Pakistan's forces were 'discovered' on the north side of the Sutlej. Once informed, Gandhi returned to New Delhi, reassigned Singh, ordered Sundarji to announce that Pakistan had moved its troops into threatening positions and dispatched additional forces to Punjab. Management of the crisis was further compromised when India's Director-General of Military Operations (DGMO) decided not to use the telephone hotline to his opposite number which had been established by the political authorities for just such an emergency.

This concentration of executive power has marked Indian foreign policy since Nehru's day: in a particularly graphic example in 1962, during the Chinese war, he placed General B. M. Kaul in command of the army and authorised action against China without consulting the military.[21] The result, according to one Indian analyst, was that '1962 was essentially a confused politician's war'.[22] This executive style was pronounced under the leadership of Nehru's daughter, Indira Gandhi, and was exemplified by her decision to conduct a nuclear test in 1974. Without raising the idea with her military advisors, 'Kitchen Cabinet' or Foreign Ministry bureaucrats, she decided to go ahead on the basis of advice from scientists responsible for the test and therefore with a stake in her decision.[23]

The unanticipated strategic implications of a decision made primarily for domestic reasons have profoundly complicated Indian defence planning ever since.

Finally, rational decision-making depends on good intelligence collection and analysis – but here again gaps undermine confidence in either country's ability to resolve confrontations peacefully. In 1987, Pakistan intercepted intelligence indicating that India intended to conclude *Brasstacks* with a thrust into Pakistan. Sundarji and Singh scoffed at the report, but the fact that Arif firmly believed it helped to escalate tension and could have prompted conflict. Further problems emerged in 1987, when India failed to notice the movement of Pakistan's reserve forces and to recognise their defensive positioning. Inadequate intelligence-gathering and misreading of intelligence obtained is a powerful reminder of the complications inherent in managing crises, reaching decisions and reducing tensions.

A disturbing intelligence failure also marked the 1990 crisis. Few senior Indian government figures felt that war was at hand, and some of the participants believed that the crisis was essentially over before US mediators arrived in May. The publication of a transcript from an academic conference in 1994, however, prompted India to reappraise what might have happened four years earlier. A US intelligence representative commented that it would take years for the whole story to emerge, that 1990 and 1987 represented cases of dreadful Indian and Pakistani intelligence, and that the Gates mission was dispatched after highest-level US intelligence assessments. These comments suggested to the authorities that something had indeed been under way which US intelligence sources had discovered – but which had escaped Indian attention.[24] In this case, bad intelligence may have had the fortunate effect of dampening the crisis, but good luck is not a substitute for good intelligence.

The failure of Indian intelligence to understand developments in Pakistan underlines the point that decision-makers may not be able to control events on the ground in a crisis. The inability to ensure good and timely intelligence undermines confidence that, in a nuclear crisis, deterrence will be stable and nuclear restraint assured. Crisis stability depends on the ability to restrain forces and to calibrate responses to enemy actions. This restraint in turn depends on being able to call the other side's bluff, or to wait him out – a difficult task under any circumstances, but particularly so if intelligence fails to monitor the other's activities adequately.

It is unlikely that any one of these factors will cause war to break out. Indeed, it is difficult to argue that deficiencies in the decision-making process *per se* cause wars. What is important is that these deficiencies make crises difficult to manage. When the two sides pose an amorphous but potentially cataclysmic threat, it is all the more critical that their relations are governed by robust decision-making mechanisms.

Conclusions

The possibility of Indo-Pakistani conflict cannot be ignored or dismissed. A number of key points bear repeating:

* Pakistan was drawn into a war it did not want in 1947–48 and began one it knew it could not win in 1965.
* Local Kashmiri insurgents almost provoked an unwanted confrontation in 1990.
* Pakistan's internal disintegration caused an international war in 1971.
* Indian fears that Pakistan would exploit Sikh grievances caused a sudden escalation in the *Brasstacks* crisis in 1987.
* Outside intervention could not prevent military defeat in 1962 and 1971.
* Highly centralised decision-making in 1987 caused important inputs to be ignored which could have averted a crisis, and then excluded the prime minister as the crisis escalated.
* Also in 1987, intelligence failure caused decision-makers to overreact; fresh failures caused them not to react at all in 1990.

These past failings must be balanced against a history of past successes and do not mean that war is likely in the future. They do, however, highlight a range of problems which should give pause to arguments that escalation will be controlled. With nuclear weapons potentially a part of the strategic landscape, deterring war in the future will be all the more important, regardless of its probability. No matter how low the risk, the cost would be unacceptably high.

Professor Robert Jervis of Columbia University has argued that although 'we should concentrate on the most likely ways in which a nuclear war could break out ... we also want to open our eyes to less probable dangers'.[25] These less probable dangers could have catastrophic consequences in South Asia.

chapter 2

Nuclear Deterrence in South Asia

Nuclear proponents argue that, although limited, Indian and Pakistani nuclear capabilities are sufficient to deter war. Two events in the continuing low-intensity conflict in Kashmir are cited as evidence.

The first is the aborted march across the Line of Control in 1992, when Pakistani troops fired on demonstrators to prevent them from gaining access to the Indian side. Pakistan's willingness to fire on Kashmiris *inside* Azad Kashmir is cited as evidence that Islamabad will not allow itself to be dragged into a war with India because of its fear of nuclear escalation.

The second piece of evidence is the contrast between India's assertive behaviour in 1965 and its restraint in Kashmir since 1989, when the current round of tensions began. In 1965, when only a few thousand Pakistan-backed infiltrators entered Indian Kashmir, New Delhi responded promptly and aggressively by pursuing them across the Line of Control. Since 1989, many more have infiltrated and terrorist activity has at times almost paralysed the state. India's response has been to deploy hundreds of thousands of troops, but at no point has it conducted hot-pursuit operations or tried to eliminate insurgent training camps on the Pakistani side of the line. India's cautious behaviour is attributed to its fear of nuclear escalation and its desire to ensure against inadvertent conflict.

These two pieces of evidence may not, however, be as clear-cut as nuclear proponents claim them to be. Although Pakistan took strong action in 1992 to maintain control of the situation, Islamabad continues to support the low-intensity conflict that almost got out of hand then, and may do so again. On the Indian side, it is by no means clear that Pakistan's nuclear capabilities have prevented escalation since 1989. India's high level of tolerance for internal disruption may have more to do with New Delhi's restraint in Kashmir than Pakistan's nuclear capability.[1] The Sikh disturbances in the Punjab in the 1980s – probably supported by Pakistan – were as serious as those in Kashmir in the 1990s. India has handled both with a combination of harsh internal repression and external restraint. Yet when the Sikh disturbances were at their height Pakistan did not pose a nuclear threat (Islamabad only announced that it had overcome the challenge of enriching uranium in February 1984). It cannot therefore be argued that Indian restraint in 1980s Punjab sprang from nuclear fears.

Before concluding that India and Pakistan's nuclear capabilities account for the cautious behaviour in Kashmir, how South Asian nuclear deterrence is conceived should be considered in more abstract terms. Understanding this may help to clarify whether Indian and Pakistani nuclear capabilities account for the restraint, and whether they will prevent war arising from the factors cited in Chapter 1.

Requirements for Nuclear Deterrence

Analysts of South Asian politics cite five elements as critical for nuclear deterrence in South Asia:

- nuclear threats require a nuclear response;
- nuclear weapons must be invulnerable to a first strike;
- delivery vehicles against high-value enemy targets must be secure;
- nuclear weapons do not replace conventional defences; and
- the nuclear capability and threat must be credible.[2]

Indian and Pakistani nuclear theorists argue that only nuclear weapons will deter enemy nuclear threats. For India, nuclear weapons are needed against China, and for Pakistan, against India. The 1962 war with China devastated Indian morale and exposed its military deficiencies, but it was only two years later, after China conducted its first nuclear test, that India began seriously to consider developing nuclear weapons. In 1964, Prime Minister Lal Bahadur Shastri enunciated what became known as the 'option policy', and India began the slow but steady progress towards an independent nuclear capability that bore fruit in a nuclear test a decade later.[3]

India's actions spoke louder than words, but the conviction that it must develop a nuclear deterrent to confront China is eloquently voiced in *Nuclear Weapons in Third World Context*, a 1981 study of nuclear deterrence and India's strategic situation.[4] Several military and civilian analysts were asked whether conventional means alone would be sufficient to deter a nuclear-armed aggressor state. They answered that only nuclear weapons would suffice. Specifically with reference to China, Indian analysts concluded that, without nuclear weapons, India would face bullying and further aggression akin to the 1962 débâcle.

Pakistan endured an even worse defeat a decade after India's war with China. The creation of Bangladesh in 1971 was a humbling experience which not only destroyed the spiritual and physical integrity of the nation, but also devastated the army. Unlike India, where conventional defeat did not provoke a nuclear response, the 1971 war convinced Pakistan that it needed a nuclear capability. In January 1972, only a month after the defeat, Zulfiqar Ali Bhutto assembled a group of scientists in Multan to launch a nuclear-weapon programme.[5] India's stunning conventional victory had provoked Pakistan's nuclear programme over two years before India conducted its nuclear test on 18 May 1974.

Because Pakistan began its nuclear programme before India's nuclear test, it cannot be argued that Pakistan initially felt that nuclear weapons were required to deter nuclear weapons. Pakistanis now argue, however, that India's nuclear programme stretches back decades before the 1974 test, and therefore that Pakistan's nuclear programme was a response to Indian nuclear proliferation, and not only the 1971 defeat.[6] Although India's civilian nuclear programme did indeed begin in the 1940s, the 1974 test marked its expansion from a civilian base to include a military focus. Furthermore, if Pakistan feared Indian nuclear weapons before the test, one would have expected to see some steps taken before 1972. Although Bhutto had supported a nuclear-weapon programme if India went ahead with one of its own, the then chairman of the Pakistan Atomic Energy Commission (PAEC), Ishrat Usmani, confirmed that Pakistan's nuclear programme had no military orientation until January 1972. Usmani resigned in January 1972 rather than follow Bhutto's orders to develop nuclear weapons, and was replaced by Munir Ahmed Khan.[7]

Pakistan now argues that the two sides should eliminate their nuclear weapons, and has proposed a number of agreements to that end. Cynics see this policy as bluff, arguing that Pakistan needs nuclear weapons to deter India's conventional superiority and makes such proposals in the conviction that India will not accept them.[8] In this way Pakistan's programme can continue under a cloak of virtue. This cynical view is unfair to Pakistan. Taking the argument at face value, then, one would conclude that, despite the beginning of Pakistan's nuclear programme in 1972, it now agrees with India that only nuclear weapons can deter a nuclear threat.

Having decided that nuclear weapons are needed, the next critical requirement for nuclear deterrence would be to develop a secure second-strike capability. This is central to classic deterrence theory, and is emphasised in an early formulation of Indian strategy, Major-General Som Dutt's seminal 1966 essay *India and the Bomb*. Dutt argued that India would need to develop an invulnerable second-strike capability requiring a 'standard of sophistication very near to that achieved by the superpowers'.[9]

Not everyone agreed with Dutt's conclusion that India would require a sophisticated command-and-control mechanism. In *Nuclear Weapons in Third World Context*, for example, it is argued that at low levels of nuclear symmetry, or when one state is in a position of nuclear inferiority, an assured second-strike capability would stabilise the relationship without an extensive command-and-control apparatus.[10] As long as neither side had confidence that all an enemy's launch sites could be eliminated, the fear of nuclear retaliation even from a slightly inferior neighbour would prevent a first strike by the stronger side, thereby ensuring strategic stability. Uncertainty over what the other side might do, rather than what it could do, would instil caution. An expensive and sophisticated command-and-control apparatus might supplement deterrence, but uncertainty alone would be sufficient to ensure that one's forces remained invulnerable.

The argument that an assured second-strike capability would create stable deterrence rests on the assumption that the side targeted by a first strike would not only have forces left with which to retaliate, but would also have the delivery means to attack high-value enemy targets. This would pose a problem for India because New Delhi lacked the ability to hit targets deep within China. To ensure stability, India would have to develop such a capability. General A. S. Vohra noted in *Nuclear Weapons in Third World Context* that if one country's high-value targets lay outside the range of the other's delivery vehicles, retaliation would be incredible and 'an environment of instability' would result.[11]

Subrahmanyam contended that in the specific case of India confronting China, Indian aircraft would bring 'enough of Southern China ... within reach for inflicting unacceptable damage'.[12] This would depend, of course, on the proportion of India's delivery vehicles, rather than the number of weapons, available after a Chinese first strike, as well as their ability to penetrate Chinese defences. Selective targeting of India's forward air bases as part of a first strike would severely damage India's ability to retaliate. The potential vulnerability of such bases, or perhaps a sense that threatening targets in south China might not deter Beijing, may have prompted India to develop the *Agni* intermediate-range ballistic missile (IRBM).

Even with nuclear weapons available and securely stored on delivery vehicles to prevent pre-emption from eliminating them, deterrence would require both sides to maintain a high level of conventional defence readiness. Doing so would keep the nuclear- use threshold high and therefore avoid instability at the sub-strategic level. Major-General Dutt argued that, although only an Indian nuclear *deterrence requires high conventional defence readiness* capability would deter China, strategic nuclear deterrence would not eliminate conventional local conflict.[13] Just as US nuclear weapons did not prevent Beijing from assisting Vietnam, India's nuclear weapons would not necessarily deter China from 'more subtle forms of trouble-making'. Dutt's insight into the strategic dilemma commonly referred to as the 'stability–instability paradox' still applies to India's relations with China, but also characterises the problem Pakistan poses through its support of insurgents in Kashmir.[14]

Sundarji later argued a similar point. Regardless of the strategic nuclear balance, conventional forces would have to be maintained to prevent either side from trying to make military gains via 'salami-slice' tactics.[15] The clear implication is that in order to prevent an anti-status quo power, knowing that escalation was deterred, from trying to gain ground at the tactical level, conventional military defence cannot be short-changed. When 'there is no possibility of substantial gains through a conventional initiative, the chances of [either side] embarking on an adventure to change the status quo is most unlikely'.[16] In a situation of extreme nuclear asymmetry, where the stronger side might consider the retaliatory threat incredible and adopt bullying tactics at the conventional level, the 'weaker' nuclear state would need to develop sufficient conventional capabilities to prevent coercion. Where the threat of nuclear retaliation might seem incredible, conventional forces would have to be able to hold their own on the battlefield.

In a similar vein, Pakistan's General Mirza Aslam Beg argued that conventional capabilities could not be reduced because doing so would lower the threshold for deterrence. He argued that 'increased penalties [i.e., US sanctions] on Islamabad could hasten a nuclear collision by lowering the threshold for a first-strike use because it would ... erode Pakistan's conventional capability'.[17]

Finally, the nuclear threat would have to be made credible. From a technical point of view, the weapons and delivery vehicles would have to function properly; from a political point of view, the other side would have to believe that they might be used. Dutt argued that a policy of nuclear deterrence meant that India would not only have to reach a clear decision about the need for nuclear weapons, but would also have to reconcile itself to the prospect of using this 'monstrous weapon'.[18] Lieutenant-General W. A. G. Pinto argued in *Nuclear Weapons in Third World Context* that stability rested on each side having a clear idea of the other's technical capability: 'one has to make known one's firm determination to retaliate, and one's veiled capability to do so, in order to create the necessary psychological impact of deterrence'.[19] This would allow each side rationally to calculate the danger it faced.

This concern was echoed by the Pakistani scholar Hasan-Askari Rizvi.[20] He argued that, although a 'kind of deterrence' existed between India and Pakistan – in the sense that both recognised that the other could make nuclear weapons but had not done so – deterrence at low levels was unstable because either side could misread signals from the other, assume it had assembled a bomb and respond accordingly. The first side would then respond by *actually* going ahead with weapon deployment, rather than keeping weapons disassembled or undeployed. The likelihood of such an action–reaction model based on misperception would be much greater in a crisis, Rizvi argued, thus increasing tensions.

Deterrence Stability in South Asia

Although the five elements listed above form a model of nuclear deterrence, it does not reflect reality in South Asia, as India and Pakistan do not meet all five criteria. For example:

- India's fears of Chinese nuclear weapons are now presumably over 30 years old, yet New Delhi has yet to produce a delivery vehicle to threaten targets deep within China.
- India's initial response to Chinese nuclear weapons was to seek a nuclear guarantee from the US and the UK.
- Pakistan claims that it is ready to give up nuclear weapons, but doing so would leave it as vulnerable as it was when it was divided in 1971.
- Indian defence spending has declined in real terms for several years, perhaps showing an indifference to regional instability.
- Both countries have fudged the issue of credibility, as India has advanced slowly since the 1974 test, while Pakistan has relied on veiled hints to give the impression that it has nuclear weapons.

What remains is a modified South Asian version of deterrence which is variously described as 'minimum', 'non-weaponised', 'recessed' and 'existential'.[21]

These descriptions collectively argue that, despite being veiled and implied, the two countries' limited nuclear capabilities eliminate factors considered to be destabilising: arms racing; nuclear testing; pre-emption; tactical targeting; prompt response; and the need to assemble weapons. To the extent that these factors are minimised or eliminated, security is thought to be increased, but it is not clear how these factors affect the likely causes of war. It appears, therefore, that India and Pakistan's limited nuclear capabilities do not reinforce stability, nor do they dampen the causes of war cited in Chapter 1. If a crisis erupts, they will not make management easier; if war breaks out, they will not reduce the likelihood of nuclear use.

A first general proposition is that minimum deterrence makes it unnecessary to match a neighbour's nuclear developments, implying that arms racing will be avoided and stability maintained.[22] Since the threatened side would fear the use of only a few weapons, not hundreds, expanding a stockpile beyond a few devices would be unnecessary. In a private discussion with the author, celebrated Pakistani scientist Dr A. Q. Khan made essentially this point, saying that if a country had five or ten nuclear weapons, it would not need to expand its stockpile to ensure its security.[23] Large stockpiles would be irrelevant, since each country would know that the threat would be taken seriously even with only a few weapons available, and would therefore avoid building more and more. Even if one side expanded its stockpile, it would not reduce the other's security, so long as the delivery vehicles remained invulnerable.

This logic appears not to affect India and Pakistan, as arms competition continues. At low levels of technical development and few weapons, India and Pakistan appear highly sensitive to each other's progress. For example, a flurry of concern met reports in late 1995 and early 1996 that India was planning a nuclear test.[24] In response, Foreign Minister Pranab Mukherjee admitted that New Delhi had planned to 'exercise the option', but added that the government was forced to postpone testing.[25] Pakistan responded by asserting that it would match any Indian test.[26] Similarly, when India was reported to have tested and then to have deployed the *Prithvi* missile, Pakistan replied that it would continue its missile developments, and tested a *Hatf 3*.[27] Although Pakistan alleges that it unilaterally halted production of highly enriched uranium (HEU) in

1989–90, India has not reciprocated (Pakistan continues to produce low-enriched uranium, perhaps hedging its bets).[28] China has also suspended production of fissile material, yet New Delhi has not followed suit.

India's competition with China also fuels Indo-Pakistani competition. Although China does not regard India in the same light as India views China, New Delhi's efforts to counter Beijing make it appear more threatening to Pakistan. The 'option' policy may have been conceived to allow India to progress far enough with its weapon and delivery programmes to feel secure against China without appearing overly threatening to Pakistan. If so, it has not succeeded: Islamabad has responded to every Indian advance with its own military developments. This vicious circle complicates relations on both sides.

Political control over the scientific community would be needed to restrain arms competition. P. R. Chari notes that, in the West, policy and strategy resulted from technical advances, and comments:

> *Regrettably, this is precisely what is also occurring in India due to the absence of sufficient thought being given to expressing its defence policy with some degree of precision and comprehensiveness. This is apparent from the lack of any mention on its nuclear and missile deployment policy.*[29]

Whether political control is now exercised – and whether those in control are informed and analytically sound in their judgements – are unanswered questions. South Africa offers an interesting comparison. There, political leaders placed tight constraints on their nuclear scientists to ensure that political factors, not scientific progress, governed strategic policy.[30] Political control of all security-related decision-making is no less critical in South Asia.

General Sundarji argues that minimum deterrence obviates the need to enhance the reliability or yield of nuclear weapons.[31] High reliability and high yield would allow a state to plan a counter-force attack that would ensure that the opponent's protected targets would be eliminated. Minimum deterrence advocates argue that hardened targets would not be attacked, making weapon improvements unnecessary. India and Pakistan appear to accept this argument, as neither has pursued an extensive testing programme to improve its weapons.

Logically, however, this argument is flawed, since high reliability could be important for counter-force as well as counter-value targeting. Redundant targeting (assigning more than one weapon per target) to compensate for poor performance might be impossible against battlefield targets, as supplies of delivery vehicles and fissile material would be limited. Even if large numbers of weapons were available, transporting them to their delivery vehicles after a nuclear strike, and then delivering them to their designated targets, would require extensive advance logistical planning. High reliability could compensate for a lack of adequate advance planning.

India and Pakistan's limited nuclear capabilities are also thought to provide stable deterrence because neither side would conduct a pre-emptive strike nor feel the need to use nuclear weapons early in a conflict.[32] However, because Pakistan believes that it needs to threaten to use nuclear weapons to counter India's conventional superiority, it refuses to sign a no-first-use agreement. That does not mean that Pakistan will attempt a pre-emptive strike, but it does make a crisis more difficult for India to manage without increasing alert levels and taking defensive precautions to ensure that its forces remain invulnerable.

Anticipating Pakistan's unwillingness to forego threatening first use, General Sundarji argued that, regardless of a declared no-first-use policy, minimum deterrence would ensure stability because a state would retain the right to 'defend itself with all means at its disposal when its very survival is at stake'.[33] This argument depends, however, on the interpretation of state survival and the pace of the conventional war. It would be pointless to use a nuclear weapon so late in a conflict as not to guarantee that the state would survive. Early use, therefore, may make sense to ensure that the other side's conventional forces could not create irreversible battlefield conditions which would make state survival impossible, and nuclear use irrelevant.[34]

Minimum deterrence also assumes that since neither side plans a first strike – logically against nuclear, military or industrial targets – both would attack only soft targets, mainly cities.[35] However, even if both sides are unlikely to conduct a pre-emptive strike against the other's nuclear, military or industrial facilities, it is not axiomatic that only cities would be targeted after the outbreak of war. Massed tank formations, narrow defiles, critical supply nodes and command-and-control centres present attractive nuclear targets, particularly for a conventionally inferior military facing battlefield reversal. Pakistani Lieutenant-Colonel Syed Anwar Mehdi argues that Pakistan's geography, 'particularly in the crucial and decisive sectors, lends itself naturally to the use of tactical nuclear weapons'.[36] A country using tactical nuclear weapons would want to be certain of the weapons' yield and delivery-vehicle accuracy to ensure the safety of its own forces, but this is not an insurmountable challenge, even in the early stages of technical development.[37] Escalating to attacks on cities may make little military sense if the course of battle might be reversed with a well-placed nuclear strike against a key military target.

General A. M. Vohra raised a related issue, noting that, in the massive overkill relationship between East and West in the Cold War, any use of nuclear weapons threatened to expand rapidly into a nuclear holocaust. In contrast, 'in a situation of low-level nuclear symmetry, the danger of a nuclear holocaust does not exist'.[38] The result, he argued, was that without the fear of widespread destruction hanging over the battlefield, low-yield nuclear weapons could be used tactically, for example, against a bridgehead. Vohra retreated from this argument, saying that 'on further reflection it will become apparent that it is probable that even in this eventuality nuclear weapons would be used against value targets'.[39]

Not only does this presume that, at low levels of technical sophistication, each side would have the ability to hit high-value targets, it fails to explain why the nuclear-holocaust argument is invalid. If India and Pakistan are unable to hit high-value targets, for example, because of delivery-vehicle limitations, deterrence may be even less stable given Vohra's point that India and Pakistan do not face a nuclear holocaust as a result of nuclear use. Limited strikes may make sense, especially at the tactical level, even with small numbers of weapons on both sides. As Vohra noted, the threat of massive overkill would not apply because of low overall numbers of weapons, low yield, unreliability or inaccurate targeting, which could reduce the fear of retaliation.

A further benefit which arguably results from maintaining limited nuclear capabilities is that, because India and Pakistan would not plan pre-emptive or early nuclear use, neither would need to place its forces on hair-trigger alert nor threaten a hair-trigger response.[40] For this to stabilise relations, however, neither side should be able to convince itself that it could mount a nuclear-decapitation strike. Command-and-control centres and the decision-making chain would need to be robust enough to survive a nuclear attack, thereby eliminating the necessity to threaten a prompt response. A vulnerable command centre might require a pre-delegated chain of command and authority to launch a nuclear retaliatory strike. This would ensure that elimination of the command centre would not create indecision nor destroy the targeted state's ability to respond promptly.

The doctrine of 'no prompt response' implies that national decision-makers would consider not only *when*, but even *if* they should respond to a nuclear attack. The attacker would assume that nuclear retaliation would result from a counter-value attack, but not necessarily from a battlefield, counter-force attack. Responding to tactical use by escalating to strikes against cities might be disproportionate and militarily counter-productive.

the doctrine of 'no prompt response'

This raises the issue of nuclear use for war-fighting. A late-response doctrine may enhance pre-war stability but, in the course of war, stability rests on expectations that nuclear escalation can be controlled. With small numbers of nuclear weapons this may be manageable, but may require significant modifications in strategic planning.

Subrahmanyam argues that controlling the conduct of war once it has been initiated, a basic postulate of war planning, could not be met in a nuclear conflict.[41] The no-prompt-response doctrine, however, implies that some measure of control would have to be maintained. How nuclear weapons are used and their effect on the battlefield raises the issue of intra-war deterrence. This implies that decisions about when and where to respond to nuclear use must be made *after* a nuclear attack. P. R. Chari notes that 'the real danger from tactical nuclear weapons arises from the psychology it engenders that nuclear war is possible'.[42] As General Vohra writes, if tactical use becomes thinkable,

> it must be assumed that both countries have developed relevant doctrine for the deployment of forces in a nuclear environment and have adequate surveillance, early warning and necessary command and control apparatus.[43]

This issue is further complicated by the introduction of SRBMs into South Asia. Nuclear-armed SRBMs would not *necessarily* force either side to adopt a prompt response or launch-on-warning doctrine, but they would make command and control during a war all the more important. A secure command-and-control centre, as well as hardened communication links to missile commands, would be required to ensure that, after the initial nuclear attack, the command authorities would be able to communicate the order to respond. Alternatively, if command, control and communications (C^3) are not secure, pre-delegation of launch authority to the SRBM missile commands, regardless of a late-response doctrine, would undermine crisis stability and might also compromise efforts to control escalation in the event of war.

A doctrine of no prompt response is thought to be stable if the two sides have not weaponised their nuclear arsenals (mating all parts of the bomb).[44] Indian Air Commodore Jasjit Singh calls this 'recessed deterrence', requiring a state to have a 'nuclear tech-nological base ... more than adequate to achieve weaponisation at short notice'.[45] The principal advantage in keeping weapons unassembled lies in the extended time needed to ready them for use, thereby keeping nuclear forces from hair-trigger status. As a crisis mounted, preparation of nuclear weapons could be observed, allowing third parties to intervene and arrest momentum.

Prior experience and published evaluations, however, suggest that neither India nor Pakistan's intelligence services would be able to monitor weaponisation activities in the depth of detail required.[46] Relying on third parties to do so would also be problematic, even with accurate, sharable intelligence. If a third party advised one country that its opponent was readying nuclear weapons and where those weapons were located, military and civilian leaders might favour a pre-emptive strike. Faced with such intelligence, there would be a risk that the crisis could not be contained and the other side convinced not to continue its preparations. Alternatively, if the state were only informed that the other side was readying its nuclear weapons, but not where, this might do little more than touch off the same weaponisation behaviour. Rather than damping down the crisis, this intelligence-sharing would propel it forward. Furthermore, a false alarm during a crisis could accelerate war preparations. It is quite easy to misread activities on the ground and to conclude that benign military movements are in fact preparations for conflict. A false intelligence signal from a third country could cause the very behaviour it was supposed to prevent.

Intelligence issues apart, handicapping both sides with a time buffer would not necessarily stabilise a crisis. Fearing that the other side had 'cheated', or was better-positioned to mobilise its forces quickly, both might work all the more feverishly to ready their forces during a crisis. Both might fear that, once the other completed its weaponisation, it would attack delivery sites, thereby preventing nuclear retaliation. Conventional weapons could be used to knock out delivery systems, although with far less expectation of success.

For a time buffer to be effective, both sides would have to conduct regular nuclear-alert exercises to allow for the confident deployment of forces in the event of a crisis. Without training, both sides would run the risk of accidents or unexpected events interfering with weaponisation. However, regular exercises would heighten tension, exacerbate fears of surprise attack and increase the possibility of false alarms. In short, separating nuclear components would not eliminate the need for strategic warning, with its attendant rise in tensions and perhaps in alert levels.[47]

Conclusions

It is difficult to conclude that nuclear weapons enhance stability. As Chari argues:

> *The conclusion that a state of bilateral nuclear deterrence now obtains in South Asia following [the 1987 and 1990] Indo-Pak crises, or that a condition of minimum nuclear*

deterrence is currently stabilising their relations, is quite premature.[48]

The acquisition of limited nuclear capabilities has not eliminated competition in missile development, fissile-material production or nuclear testing. India and Pakistan remain sensitive to each other's developments and continue to expand technically. Meanwhile, Indian competition with China fuels Indo-Pakistani competition.

The desire to test new weapons, whether to enhance reliability or to improve yield, has also not been eliminated. India's apparent interest in further testing suggests that its scientists may not be content with the current situation. If the military were involved in nuclear planning, the interest in testing could indicate that military requirements have not yet been met and that further enhancements were required. However, this is unlikely as India's military provides no General Staff Quality Review (GSQR) to the scientific community for nuclear weapons, although it does so for every conventional weapon in its arsenal.[49]

Limited nuclear capabilities have also failed to eliminate first-strike options, particularly during war. The clandestine nature of the two countries' programmes is sufficient to deprive either of confidence that it could successfully eliminate the other's nuclear infrastructure. But the implied threat each poses to the other's high-value targets, such as cities, does not mean that only cities would be targeted if war broke out. Limited nuclear capabilities do not affect the likelihood of nuclear use during war. Indeed, in order to exploit the benefit of avoiding prompt response, command-and-control capabilities must be developed and maintained.

Beyond what acquiring limited nuclear capability has *not* done, what it *has* done is raise the possibility that nuclear weapons may be used in a future war. They may be used only in a counter-value role – although it is possible that they would be employed for war-fighting. It could be argued that command-and-control mechanisms make nuclear war-fighting more likely, and therefore ought to be avoided. But without such mechanisms, it may also be more difficult to avoid widespread devastation if war occurs.

The development and possible deployment of ballistic missiles exacerbates these destabilising factors. As the two sides compete in missile technology, the ability to avoid prompt response is reduced. In addition, refraining from assembling weapons becomes a risk when the other side is capable of attacking launch sites with SRBMs which cannot be defended against. Fighter aircraft, which must overcome air defences before reaching their targets, do not pose the same level of threat. Furthermore, to ensure that a launch-on-warning policy – which may result from SRBM deployment – is not adopted, command and control must be enhanced.

The belief that India and Pakistan's limited nuclear capabilities have created stable deterrence may lead to complacency in thinking about what to do if war breaks out. The two sides may be deterred from beginning a war, but more because of their political disinclination to do so and their conventional inability to achieve plausible political objectives.[50] Limited nuclear capabilities play a relatively small role in establishing stable relations – but significantly raise the costs if war breaks out. The following chapters will consider how nuclear stability may be enhanced and the costs of war decreased by paying greater attention to the management of nuclear weapons and the improvement of bilateral ties.

chapter 3

Enhancing Nuclear Stability

Chapter 1 concluded that, although war may currently be unlikely in South Asia, problems persist which could cause conflict. Chapter 2 concluded that the confidence of many in India and Pakistan that limited nuclear capabilities will bring stability may be misplaced and may lead to complacency in thinking about what should be done in the event of war. If war breaks out, both sides will want a choice between suicide and surrender – but the shadow of nuclear weapons may leave few other options.

The decision to develop a nuclear capability requires weapons to be treated as more than symbols; it is safer to consider whether to use them before a potentially cataclysmic decision is forced by a crisis or war. India and Pakistan can consider certain steps which would offer options to respond to a nuclear provocation without launching retaliatory strikes or, at a minimum, causing widespread destruction. This would require closer attention to an area which has received relatively little attention: command and control.[1] Peacetime steps to improve command and control may have destabilising effects if seen by the enemy as preparations for war. However, failure to take those steps may mean that, in the event of war, nuclear use is more likely and more destructive.

Preventing or limiting the use of nuclear weapons requires their careful management. Professors Ashton Carter, John Steinbruner and Charles Zraket note the relative inattention paid to this area:

An imbalance exists in the study of security in the nuclear
age. The process of managing the arsenals is less discussed
and less familiar than either the weapons themselves or the
doctrinal logic used to define their purposes.[2]

This is no less true for India and Pakistan than it is for the five declared nuclear-weapon states. Given that minimum deterrence says little about what will be deterred, or how stability will be maintained during crisis or war, it is important for India and Pakistan to consider how nuclear operations may be managed, and what steps might be taken to reduce the likelihood of loss of control, escalation and nuclear use.

Command and Control in Peacetime

Pakistan and India appear to maintain tight control over nuclear components, ensuring that they cannot be quickly deployed. This conforms to the argument that minimum deterrence provides stability because weapons are unassembled. Pakistan's Munir Ahmed Khan has written that, although Pakistan has never possessed a nuclear device, 'the government had taken the necessary measures and precautions to ensure that no one could make or assemble one, much less go to the stage of having a usable nuclear weapon'.[3]

Khan chose his words carefully. The US was legally bound to stop aid if it determined that Pakistan possessed a 'nuclear device'. Pakistan objected to the US definition of possession as implied by the 1990 Pressler Amendment, which restricted aid if Pakistan crossed the nuclear threshold:

A state may possess a nuclear explosive device, and yet
maintain it in unassembled form ... [but] the fact that a state
does not have an assembled device would not ... necessarily
mean that it does not possess a device.[4]

In other words, Khan implied that Pakistan had manufactured weapon parts, but kept them unassembled in an effort to comply with the conditions for continued US aid. This is consistent with several more-or-less official government statements to the effect that

Pakistan possessed elements which, if put together, would become a nuclear weapon.[5] Pakistan interpreted its behaviour as consistent with Washington's conditions for continued aid. Making a nuclear device (assembling all the components) was, as Khan put it, 'the line not to be crossed'.[6] Pakistan evidently kept the components separate primarily for political, rather than strategic, technical or safety, reasons.

This practice would also ensure command and control. This seems to be the import of Khan's statement that the Pakistani government ensured that 'no one could make or assemble one'. Weapon components may be kept separated to ensure executive control. The nature of that executive control is unclear, but with the Pakistani Army playing an important role in managing national affairs, it is likely that it also has significant responsibilities for the weapon components that have been manufactured.

The Indian situation is more obscure because its nuclear programme is not subject to annual certification for US aid purposes, and Indian leaders have never found it necessary to make elliptical comments about weapon components, rarely venturing beyond general statements about the programme. Despite the military's exclusion from nuclear planning, General Sundarji warned that 'the subcontinent cannot be assumed to be one-sided, with Pakistan having weaponised and India not having done so'.[7] The 1974 test demonstrated that India *could* manufacture and assemble components for a bomb, but whether additional devices or device components have been made, and how they are stored, has not been publicly discussed.

The armed forces do not appear to control either assembled weapons or weapon parts. Dr V. Arunachalam, a former senior science adviser to the government, stated that the military 'would not be and has not been told how many nuclear weapons India might have nor was it told in peacetime how nuclear weapons would be used in war'.[8] This view finds a number of echoes: Brigadier Vijai Nair argues that integrating 'the military into the national nuclear strategy ... needs to be done with a sense of urgency', while Gujral has commented that, while foreign minister in the V. P. Singh government of 1989–90, he was never briefed on the status of India's nuclear weapons.[9]

With the Indian military, and also probably the foreign-policy community, excluded from the peacetime nuclear chain of command, the Department of Atomic Energy (DAE) presumably would retain control of weapon components, much as did the US Atomic Energy Commission in the 1950s.[10] To ensure that a fully assembled device did not fall into the wrong hands, and to avoid extensive additional policing of the area where assembled weapons would be stored, India may also keep weapon components separated from each other. The military stores fusing mechanisms for conventional ordnance apart from explosives; a similar practice may be followed in the nuclear area.[11] The task for a terrorist – or anyone else attempting to seize nuclear weapons – would be complicated if separated components were held in different storage areas.

integrating the military into nuclear strategy

Separating nuclear components also decreases the risk of accidents. The issue of safety and security has always been of great concern in the US, but may also prove to be important elsewhere. With US nuclear weapons housed in submarines, the problem of a launch-tube breach causing the nuclear-armed missile to be immersed in water prompted concerns about safety; fears that a delivery vehicle might crash, subjecting the weapons on board to intense jet-fuel fire, contributed to concern about the volatility of the explosive charge and therefore to the development of insensitive high explosive (IHE); concerns about keeping nuclear weapons secure in Europe while maintaining civilian control over their use prompted the development of permissive action link (PAL) technology.[12]

Component separation would reduce these dangers in India and Pakistan. But once a crisis develops and steps to assemble a weapon are taken, safety issues arise. Weapons may be dropped while being loaded, subjected to electrical interference, seized during transfer (by disaffected military personnel or others), fired prematurely once launch authority is transferred or exposed to fire during conventional hostilities. Both Indian and Pakistani leaders may therefore consider safety guidelines, incorporate IHE into designs, or install PALs on stockpiled components to ensure that control is maintained and stability assured.

Nuclear Planning: Doctrine, Response and Warning

If, as Munir Khan and Arunachalam imply, Pakistan and India maintain peacetime control of nuclear weapons by keeping components separated and/or away from delivery vehicles, *unauthorised* use is unlikely. It is not clear, however, at which point or under what conditions *authorised* use would be allowed. The decision to retain nuclear capabilities implies that a decision may have to be taken authorising or foregoing use. Decision-makers in New Delhi and Islamabad should not be lulled into thinking that minimum deterrence is sufficient to prevent this situation from arising. Even stable minimum deterrence would not prevent crises and possibly conflict; thinking about nuclear planning sooner rather than later will increase the likelihood that reason rather than panic dictates the outcome of a nuclear confrontation. Both countries must address issues such as doctrine, alternative response options, alerts, early warning and intelligence.

India and Pakistan have apparently made no major effort to adapt their strategic policies to the acquisition of nuclear capabilities.[13] Analysts in both countries maintain that neither side is irrational enough to use nuclear weapons, but this is no substitute for integrating political interests with the military means to defend them.[14] Nuclear weapons are seen – even by South Asia's nuclear proponents – to have only political value, but if they are treated as little more than symbols they will not only fail to prevent war, they will also make it more costly. Professor Barry Posen notes that because resources are scarce, 'the most appropriate military means should be selected to achieve the political ends in view'.[15]

However, the connection between nuclear weapons in India and Pakistan and specific political objectives in the event of war is unclear. It is not clear whether either country has decided on the size and mix of its stockpile, but relatively small numbers of weapons may establish boundaries on strategic doctrine. Low numbers of weapons make an extended nuclear war unlikely as both countries would have to assume that some weapons might fail, some delivery vehicles might not reach their destination and some targets might be missed. With small numbers, Pakistan could not expect to achieve victory with nuclear weapons alone, and a portion of the stockpile would need to be retained to terminate the war on favourable grounds.

Even after a nuclear exchange, leaders on both sides would want to terminate the conflict without further nuclear use. Intra-war deterrence is difficult to calculate as much would depend on the damage done, the disposition of forces in the field, the involvement of third-party intermediaries and other, unforeseen, factors. Neither side may therefore be able to use many nuclear weapons in a conflict. An alternative strategy may be to brandish the weapons by conducting a nuclear demonstration, but, depending on the conduct of the war, this may serve only to deplete the stockpile while escalating tensions.

Given the inherent limits on the use of nuclear weapons, it would help if India and Pakistan considered how they might be used to achieve political objectives before a crisis forced the issue. Thinking about how to end a nuclear confrontation on terms that serve the national interest ought to precede conflict rather than emerge from it.

India and Pakistan's invulnerable nuclear capabilities make it unlikely that either would plan a pre-emptive attack. Planning a nuclear strike at the beginning of a war might be tempting if it eliminated the other side's decision-making apparatus. The war would still have to be won on the battlefield or at the negotiating table, however. Escalation at the outset would compromise hopes that an initial battlefield advantage would lead to a cease-fire and a diplomatic resolution – a strategy Pakistan might hope to adopt.

Planning a large-scale nuclear attack at the end of a war might accomplish little beyond revenge and would amount to using the most powerful weapon when it would have least effect in achieving the political or military objectives that may have caused the war in the first place. If Pakistan planned to attack New Delhi in the closing minutes of a war it was about to lose, it might make little sense for India to retaliate against Pakistani cities – a move as morally indefensible as the initial attack, militarily inconsequential and potentially provocative or destabilising *vis-à-vis* a third party such as China. A more nuanced response would be needed for India to end hostilities with Pakistan, while remaining on a war footing with China.

If it appears unlikely that nuclear weapons will be used for pre-emption or revenge, India and Pakistan must consider how to respond to some form of war-fighting. Pakistan may strike in the midst of a war, when it feared that the tide of battle was turning in India's favour and that outside help was either unavailable or would be ineffective in achieving a cease-fire.[16] Responding to battlefield or tactical nuclear use with a counter-value attack against cities would not necessarily further India's strategic objectives. A limited response might be more successful to show resolve, to respond to public pressure to retaliate, to bolster soldiers' morale, or to reverse setbacks on the battlefield.

Controlling the response in this way would give Pakistan the opportunity to recognise that a larger attack could have been launched, and could yet be unless both sides de-escalated. More importantly, both sides would want to retain the option of terminating the conflict without their forfeiting military and political objectives.

To maintain control over the progress of the war and to suit the response to the attack, India would need to consider alternative options before war broke out. Targets could be identified in advance to ensure that they could be hit and that they could not be relocated after hostilities began. Some targets might be selected for attack to convey resolve, but to limit damage in order to encourage reciprocal restraint rather than escalation. Such targets could include the nuclear infrastructure (although this is prohibited by India and Pakistan's agreement not to attack each other's nuclear facilities), conventional mili *a response to war-fighting must be considered* tary bases or forces, command centres or economic targets. The choice would depend on the scale of the provocation. In response to a nuclear strike, a conventional attack on an economic target, such as a dam, could cause greater damage than a nuclear attack against a military base. No response at all is also an option, but if these possibilities are not evaluated prior to hostilities, the response selected during the conflict could undermine, rather than serve, strategic objectives. Avoiding or deferring nuclear war-planning runs the risk that war could escalate without serving a useful political end.

India and Pakistan may require alternative response options because the provocation may be more ambiguous than a direct nuclear strike. For example, a handling or loading accident or design flaw could cause a device to detonate. The national commander would need to determine that a nuclear blast on his own territory was the result of an accident, not an enemy strike, so as not to respond with a retaliatory attack.

Loading a nuclear weapon on to an aeroplane or missile during a crisis – assuming it were detected – would be an escalation, but would not necessarily require a nuclear response. The intent to launch a nuclear attack could not be ignored, although India may want to respond by threatening punishment, yet stop short of nuclear use. Such a response would be difficult to calibrate in the midst of a crisis, particularly if it were assumed, or intelligence indicated, that a second delivery vehicle was being readied for attack. A nuclear weapon might be fired, but might fail to detonate, detonate prematurely or land as a dud. Such an attack could not be ignored – although it might not justify massive nuclear retaliation. Again, deciding on an appropriate response in the heat of war would be difficult.

Perhaps the greatest advantage of pre-planned responses is that they would be subject to careful scrutiny. This might reassure the national decision-maker that he or she need not promptly escalate regardless of the provocation. A range of options would be useful to avoid presenting the leader with a war plan that had not been properly and fully examined. Military leaders may scrupulously observe the separation of civilian from military authority during peacetime. When conflict breaks out, however, war plans may satisfy military contingencies, but make negotiation impossible. Advance planning and extensive inter-agency review would allow greater latitude if the time came to decide between using nuclear weapons or peacefully resolving hostilities.

These issues have almost certainly been discussed in terms of conventional war, but they may not have been raised in anticipation of a possible nuclear confrontation. Based on Gujral and Arunachalam's statements, it appears that neither the Indian Foreign Ministry nor the uniformed military has been consulted on this sensitive – but critical – issue.

India and Pakistan also face significant demands for improved strategic and tactical warning. At some point in a crisis they may decide to put nuclear forces on alert, prompting a variety of steps by a large number of personnel to ready weapons for firing. India's military budget has not been maintained in real terms over the past decade, with training especially hard hit.[17] Insufficient training could create serious problems or even chaos. Moving weapon components from storage areas to delivery vehicles and launch positions might appear to the other side as preparation for an offensive – undermining efforts to resolve a crisis peacefully. Even more routinised movements would be escalatory. In a crisis, it is vital that both sides are convinced that opposition field activity is well rehearsed and tightly controlled. If an alert exercise were conducted for the first time during a crisis, decision-making in prior confrontations suggests that it would convey precisely the opposite impression.

It would be difficult to disguise this activity, thus delaying training and then hoping to avoid detection would be unlikely to succeed. In India, the military would become involved, and security increased. Transport systems would become congested and public debate could lead to civil disruption. Loading procedures could be problematic if nuclear weapons were housed on *Prithvis*. Moving the missiles from storage bunkers to launch positions means fuelling them on-site, a potentially dangerous procedure unless thoroughly rehearsed. A weapon could be loaded before missiles were transferred to the field, but fuelling with a weapon on board would raise safety issues. Alternatively, a weapon could be loaded after fuelling, requiring a

strategic and tactical warning must be improved

high-security convoy to accompany each one during transfer to its launch base. To exploit the *Prithvi's* mobility, the fuelled and armed missile would finally have to be relocated to a pre-designated launch site. Under optimal conditions, this would be challenging for the personnel involved. Without careful training, it could be disastrous in a crisis.

For Pakistan, many of the same activities would be equally difficult to conceal. Moving weapon components to missiles, presumably assembling the weapons on-site, loading them quickly and deploying missiles to launch sites would be especially dangerous without careful training.

Deployments such as these during periods of high tension would render delivery vehicles, particularly aeroplanes, vulnerable. A national decision-maker might be deterred from launching a pre-emptive nuclear strike against the opponent's nuclear infrastructure, but a conventional attack against a soft battlefield target could be difficult to resist. As it is extremely difficult to locate a mobile missile once it leaves its storage area, both sides would be all the more sensitive to the other's preparations in times of crisis. Deciding whether to attack a storage site before the delivery vehicle gained the advantage provided by mobility would depend on each side's political and military objectives, whether the crisis could be contained, uncertainty over the other side's behaviour under stress and a willingness to take risks. These factors should be thought through well before a crisis to avoid hasty and possibly unwarranted escalation.

Neither side would want to begin war preparations without unambiguous information about its opponent's activities. However, Professor Desmond Ball's study of Indian and Pakistani signals intelligence (SIGINT) capabilities suggests that neither side can rely on them to provide real-time monitoring.[18] Less is known of their human intelligence (HUMINT) capabilities, but HUMINT is notoriously difficult to acquire and even more difficult to assess. National decision-makers would therefore almost certainly want to verify a HUMINT warning during a crisis via technical means. In cases where the SIGINT did not confirm the HUMINT, photographic intelligence from aerial or space reconnaissance might remove key uncertainties. However, the extent of each side's access to surveillance platforms is unclear.

Without better access to accurate and timely intelligence, both sides will be operating in the dark. This increases their vulnerability to attack and restricts their ability to assess the other side's activities, calibrate responses and navigate safely through a crisis. One burden of acquiring nuclear weapons and ballistic missiles is that countries need to be prepared to take such steps. Making threats without being able to monitor their effects increases the cost of failure without increasing security.

The importance of strategic intelligence, even in a recessed or non-weaponised nuclear confrontation, is clear, but acquiring intelligence is only the first step. Interpreting it and resolving discrepancies between sources can be contentious and inconclusive – particularly under crisis conditions. This degree of intelligence synthesis and analysis appears to be lacking in India and Pakistan.[19]

Strategic intelligence would also be needed to assess damage in the event of a limited nuclear strike and to plan an appropriate response. Damage assessment is difficult in conventional wars, when a decision needs to be reached based on a variety of factors, including the availability of remaining forces, which targets no longer require firepower or manpower, and which enemy positions have been taken or threaten to break through. Warning and communication systems are all the more vital if a nuclear weapon has detonated, but deciding on a suitable response would be critical for war to be concluded with military or political objectives intact.

Command and Control in War

Command and control must be maintained during hostilities to ensure that nuclear use, if it cannot be avoided, does not become indiscriminate. Khan's statement about the separation of nuclear-weapon components suggests that Pakistan maintains assertive control (i.e., central authorities maintain control over the weapons). Based on Arunachalam's comments, India does the same.

This peacetime practice may, however, meet with problems in wartime, when both sides would have to consider when to delegate weapon control. Professor Peter Feaver of Duke University has noted that the US shifted from an assertive to a delegative command posture as crises loomed.[20] Although a delegative posture means that commanders are not caught unawares in the event of war, deterrence stability depends on both sides' leaders remaining in firm control of their forces (i.e., in an assertive posture) – even in a crisis. India and Pakistan may be able to maintain control even after delegating authority to a field commander, or they may never delegate authority to the field level. But unless the nuclear capability continues to be treated as a political weapon after the outbeak of war, additional military officers would become involved, diminishing executive control. A high premium must therefore be placed on training officers, conducting psychological screening and protecting the command system from disruption.

Arunachalam has claimed that if New Delhi went up 'in a mushroom cloud', a theatre commander would open a safe and follow the instructions for nuclear retaliation contained therein.[21] This suggests that release codes are in place (in the 'safe') and that pre-delegation of command has taken place. Given that the military is excluded from nuclear planning, this implies that it is prepared to follow commands issued by a civilian authority without considering the strategic or tactical utility of the order.

Arunachalam's statement also raises the issue of where the command instructions are located (where is the 'safe'?), and how they are secured. During a conflict it would be necessary to locate the orders and authenticate them in the absence of a national commander. With the military barred from strategic planning, its authority in a crisis may be challenged at field level. A command to fire nuclear weapons could be disobeyed if a local commander were unable to confirm what had happened at headquarters or the fate of the national commander. Without a robust command-and-control structure, India could be caught off-guard without recourse to authoritative decision-makers.

A further problem is the integration of the armed services. In past wars, little inter-service coordination was evident.[22] With the military excluded from strategic nuclear planning, the army and air force would be hard-pressed to manage a ground war that included readying nuclear-capable delivery vehicles. It would be imperative that air delivery of weapons be closely coordinated with ground-attack forces. If, with Indian ground forces overrunning Pakistani troops and advancing rapidly on key cities, Islamabad launched a nuclear strike, New Delhi would want to be sure that a retaliatory strike by the air force did not endanger its own forces.

As a crisis develops, the air force in particular must be certain which equipment to reserve for nuclear delivery.[23] Designated aircraft must be properly rigged to carry and release weapons and to fly sufficient distances, with sufficient loiter capability and pro-tection, either to be recalled or diverted to a new target. These plans cannot be laid at the last minute after New Delhi has been lost in a 'mushroom cloud'. As the armed forces are excluded from decision-making, they may prepare delivery-related logistical details independently – a difficult task without knowledge of a weapon's dimensions, weight, tolerance and robustness. On the other hand, civilians may plan a similar wartime response without consulting the military. Again, important details could be overlooked.

Maintaining firm control *before* a war is important in convincing the enemy that a nuclear attack would not come out of the blue. But both sides would also need to be certain that the same control would apply *throughout* a crisis or war. Unauthorised nuclear use must be prevented at all costs, particularly in the light of the 1995 coup attempt in Pakistan and the country's history of military seizures of power.[24] The impression that the other side is not integrated internally could be a strong incentive to act first, particularly if, for example, India felt that a Pakistani civilian prime minister was unable to assert authority over the military chief – as may have occurred in spring 1990. That confrontation did not reach a crisis stage. Had war broken out, New Delhi's leaders may have feared that, without robust command and control over Pakistan's nuclear weapons, its generals may have taken action not authorised by the civilian leadership. India might have been tempted to act preemptively to avoid a more widespread war. Pakistani confidence in the integrity of its command-and-control structure, even under highly delegated, crisis-driven conditions, might not be enough to reassure India; failing to ensure that command and control are well in hand runs the risk of escalating a crisis or short-circuiting negotiations which could resolve it.

Conclusions

Minimum deterrence says little about how nuclear war may be avoided or its consequences limited if war breaks out. Thinking through the problems associated with nuclear management and operations would increase the likelihood that war does not end in catastrophe. Continuing to defer the issue increases the risk of a less than optimal decision should a crisis occur.

Improved nuclear-operation management need not push India and Pakistan into overt nuclear postures. Many of these steps could be completed in the same manner in which the two countries developed their nuclear capabilities. The politically convenient argument that both countries retain the capability to develop nuclear weapons, but have not yet done so, is not compromised, nor are its benefits forfeit. The advantages of deniability for an Indian or Pakistani leader include the space to slow programmes down and the maintenance of political control over the pace of nuclear development away from the glare of public attention. The benefits of partial visibility include enhanced security through the ability to threaten the enemy and independence from the global non-proliferation regime.

Although improvements to nuclear-operation management could be made without extensive public attention, they may dent confidence that war is unlikely; they would also be financially costly and technically challenging. It might also be difficult to convince politicians responsible for budget allocation that these measures are needed. Complementing unilateral operational measures with bilateral diplomatic initiatives would enhance stability and may better address the insecurities that drove India and Pakistan's nuclear programmes in the first place.

chapter 4

Stability and Diplomacy

Improved management of nuclear weapons could improve crisis management and increase the chances that India and Pakistan would be able to end a conflict with minimal destruction, even if nuclear weapons were used. Nuclear weapons and strategy have a logic of their own, but they do not deal with the underlying causes of conflict in South Asia. Exploring the diplomatic possibilities to reduce the likelihood of war is at least as important as studying strategic logic.

Sir Michael Howard argues that deterrence includes a mix of reassurance and accommodation, and should not focus exclusively on nuclear capabilities. Subrahmanyam notes that deterrence 'unless vigorously counter-vailed by improvements in political relations tends to sustain distrust and suspicion'.[1] Diplomatic efforts can provide reassurance and accommodation, and may offer as sound a basis for stabilising nuclear deterrence as improved weapons' management.

Substantial attention has been paid in recent years to developing CSBMs – even though they have not had a history of success in South Asia. Two CSBMs, military hotlines and advance notice of exercises, were in place at the time of the *Brasstacks* crisis in 1987, but the exercise was planned and conducted without as full a disclosure of its size and direction as Pakistan expected. Fearing that the exercise had ulterior motives, Pakistan countered by reposi-tioning its troops; India, misinterpreting the move, responded with further troop movements and an escalatory spiral took shape. As the crisis got under way, neither country's DGMO used the hotline.[2] This neglect of arrangements designed to dampen crises underscores the critical point: that confidence-building measures may be useless in a crisis fuelled by mistrust, undermining confidence that deterrence will be made more stable by adding new measures.

Many in South Asia view CSBMs as hypocritical and poorly disguised Western efforts to restrain India and Pakistan's nuclear programmes. India feels that such measures parallel nuclear-proliferation issues. India argues that it needs its nuclear option because of the threat from China and because the five nuclear-weapon states continue to hold nuclear weapons. India is therefore reluctant to treat the nuclear issue broadly, and CSBMs specifically, as though they only affected the subcontinent. India's willingness to discuss nuclear issues is premised on establishing multilateral negotiations, including China in particular, but also the rest of the world, on a global disarmament agreement. In India's view, global confidence-building measures – such as the Nuclear Non-Proliferation Treaty (NPT) and the Comprehensive Test Ban Treaty (CTBT) – do little more than legitimise nuclear weapons and allow continued weapon improvements by the technologically advanced nuclear-weapon states. Extending those global agreements or CSBMs to South Asia, so the argument goes, does nothing to reduce global insecurity and only demonises India and Pakistan.[3]

Pakistan sees CSBMs in a more favourable light. Pakistani discussions of nuclear proliferation frequently mention such measures, which Islamabad has proposed for a decade to reduce tension and to manage nuclear rivalry.[4] Although Pakistan shares some of India's misgivings about global norms, it has traditionally relied on outside actors to balance the scales in South Asia, and is therefore prepared to accept constraints in order to avoid becoming isolated and being left to its own devices.

The aversion many in South Asia feel towards CSBMs may be the result of their sheer volume and popularity in the West, as well as the awareness that they were not notably effective between the US and the Soviet Union. Borrowing from Winston Churchill, never has such a range of CSBMs been proposed by so many for so few. Yet without some attention to the diplomatic side of the ledger, the risk of confrontation and misperception increases. The second round of foreign-secretary meetings in June 1997 was a promising beginning. The creation of discussion groups means that it may now be possible for India and Pakistan to resolve a range of disagreements and begin their second 50 years on a better footing than they began their first.

Given the patchy history of diplomatic engagement in South Asia, some initiatives may be unfeasible, either because the positions are by now hardened or the issues too contentious. However, certain issues may be so dangerous that they cannot be ignored. Based on a combination of risk and feasibility, four categories of diplomatic engagement can be described:

- A problem is considered to be *high risk* if ignoring it will make conflict worse.
- *Low risk* implies that, if a problem is ignored, little danger will result.
- *High feasibility* does not assume that leaders on either side are ready to rush into an agreement, but simply that, because it will not impinge on national security, they should perhaps keep a more open mind.
- *Low feasibility* means that an issue has such high symbolic content that it may not be open for discussion.

India and Pakistan have already taken the most important first step in resuming official dialogue.[5] With a range of contentious issues now on the table, the search for diplomatic solutions can be expanded.

High Risk, High Feasibility

The most pressing concern is the prospect that SRBMs will be deployed. It would be best if they were not developed at all, but that may require reversing steps which have already been taken. India has moved forward with the production (and perhaps the deployment) of the *Prithvi*, and is developing the *Agni*;

SRBMs are the most pressing concern

Pakistan has worked on a short-range missile, the *Hatf* 1 and 2, and has reportedly imported M-11s from China. At least one Pakistani has argued that Pakistan may have to develop a longer-range missile.[6] Although the missile issue is contentious, the military disutility of SRBMs may offer greater prospects for success in negotiations in this area than might be expected. The high risk of doing nothing makes it vital that the issue is addressed.

The first order of business for the two countries must be to limit SRBMs. This requires national leaders to invest significant political capital to avert sliding into dangerous competition. As noted earlier, technical advances opening up new strategic possibilities can strongly drive arms-racing, needlessly complicating the diplomatic process. South Africa's political control over technical developments may be a useful guideline for India and Pakistan. Both countries are in a position to constrain their scientists, but the opportunity may not last long if missile competition is ignored.

Military contingencies also argue in favour of limiting SRBMs. From a military point of view, it is difficult to understand why India chose to develop the *Prithvi*.[7] As a mobile, liquid-fuelled missile, it will be cumbersome to manage in the field and will be a tempting target. In addition, it will achieve relatively little in military terms unless it is armed with a nuclear weapon. India has argued that the *Prithvi* will be conventionally armed and should therefore not be of great concern for strategic stability. But almost any ballistic missile is nuclear-capable, depending on the design of the nuclear weapon. In private moments, some Pakistanis may admit their belief that India is not yet ready to mount a nuclear weapon on the *Prithvi*.[8] However, the high cost, limited range and questionable accuracy of the *Prithvi* make arming it with conventional weapons implausible from Islamabad's point of view. Most Pakistani analysts assume that, sooner or later, India will arm it with nuclear weapons.

The *Prithvi*'s development may therefore force Pakistan to assemble nuclear weapons, adopt launch-on-warning procedures and expand its nuclear arsenal. These steps would put India in extreme danger, yet the *Prithvi* returns few military benefits. Pakistan can ill-afford to ignore it, but an attempt to match its development or deployment with Pakistani SRBMs could sacrifice negotiating flexibility, give India an excuse for more extensive deployments, and complicate relations with the US. Both sides have an interest in avoiding war, but fielding SRBMs would endanger the principal advantage of minimum deterrence: the long fuse on crises afforded when nuclear components are separated from each other and kept away from delivery vehicles.

Prithvi offers India very little military help against China, as it does little more than threaten Tibet. This might make sense for attacks on Chinese missile sites New Delhi claims are located there, but that would presume that India was considering a first strike against targets which at best play a supporting role in China's strategic nuclear threat against India.[9] If armed with conventional weapons, the *Prithvi* might conceivably have some battlefield utility, but that is doubtful and comes at an extremely high per-unit price.

India has denied reports that it has moved *Prithvis* near the Pakistani border. In Pakistan's view, the *Prithvi*'s mobility means that, even if kept from the border, it would be no less of a threat. Missile mobility aims to avoid detection and to allow swift re-deployment. Moreover, the 250-kilometre-range Air Force version of the *Prithvi* brings virtually all potential targets in Pakistan into easy striking range. Even at 250km, few Chinese targets are brought into range, meaning that the missile would be most useful against Pakistan. If it is not a second-strike weapon, and it cannot threaten China, Pakistanis can only conclude that it is aimed exclusively at them.

If the SRBM programmes cannot be reversed, it may be possible to increase security in another way. The two sides could provide verification that SRBMs were not configured to carry nuclear weapons. India claims that the *Prithvi* will be armed only with conventional weapons; the safety and logistical complications cited above suggest that it might be dangerous to do otherwise. Pakistan denies reports that M-11s are either in-country or being deployed. Verifying that a missile, whose existence is denied, does not carry nuclear weapons makes confidence-building difficult to say the least. But former Pakistani chief of army staff Mirza Aslam Beg, departing from the official line, claimed in 1993 that M-11s were not needed for nuclear-weapon delivery since 'we have F-16s for that'.[10] Comments such as this may not boost Indian confidence in Pakistani plans, but they may offer a point of departure for reducing the destabilising effect of SRBMs.

Regardless of Pakistani behaviour, India may want to provide verification unilaterally if decision-makers conclude that doing so would enhance India's security. It is in India's interests that Pakistan does not feel that it has to use nuclear weapons early in a war, as it might do if India were able to use a nuclear-tipped *Prithvi* to attack Pakistani delivery sites. Making it clear to Pakistan that the *Prithvi* was not able to carry a nuclear weapon, and that Pakistan's launch sites were not threatened, could significantly enhance stability.

Although the missile issue threatens to undermine South Asian relations and must be given highest priority, it might also be possible for the two sides to consider a second area for negotiation – reducing conventional forces.[11] Again, the China issue confounds relations between India and Pakistan, but New Delhi's political leaders can cite improved relations with Beijing over the past two years in defence of any decision to scale down forces against Pakistan.[12] Although engagement with Pakistan on this issue is politically sensitive – as are so many Indo-Pakistani disputes – it is a confidence-building measure that could be launched unilaterally. This would be consistent with the Gujral Doctrine, which neither expects nor demands reciprocity on every issue.[13] It would be a relatively less painful move simply because both sides have larger armies than they need or want. Manpower is the most expensive part of a defence budget, and a reduction in forces would therefore bring the added benefit of saving money.

Low Risk, High Feasibility

India and Pakistan disagree on a variety of issues which pose fewer risks in their strategic relations. To build a habit of trust, it might be helpful to address a number of non-controversial issues which do not impinge on national security. Building trust and an expectation of cooperation rather than belligerence may be the most important legacy of Prime Ministers Gujral and Sharif. Progress on softer topics could therefore set the stage for more intensive discussion of harder security issues.

The possible agreement that Pakistan should sell India its excess energy is an example of the way in which economic progress can engender goodwill and break down old prejudices.[14] Other areas for cooperation on energy matters could include joint research on energy needs and supplies, and progress on a proposed natural-gas pipeline along Pakistan's coast. Economic-development proposals concerning trade, investment and protected markets could also be addressed.

In addition, it would make sense to improve hotlines to ensure that they cannot be circumvented or ignored as they were in 1987, to begin military exchanges or joint exercises and to seek a solution to the long-running Siachen Glacier dispute over an undemarcated portion of Kashmir. Neither side is willing to admit that Siachen has no strategic importance, but at the same time neither is willing to lose face by unilaterally removing its troops from the area.[15] The issue is ripe for third-party mediation because forming a joint commission to discuss withdrawal and demarcation need not compromise Indian and Pakistani views on the future of Kashmir. Troops could be replaced by sensors and remote technical reconnaissance, allowing for a face-saving solution and eliminating a source of tension. The Siachen dispute is unlikely to provoke war, but a resolution could symbolise a new approach in Indo-Pakistani relations.

economic progress can engender goodwill

On the nuclear front, another low-risk but feasible agreement may be possible. India has proposed a no-first-use agreement. For Pakistan to agree not to use nuclear weapons would be tantamount to saying it did not need nuclear weapons for deterrence at all. A statement that it would only use nuclear weapons first if its national integrity were threatened could, however, reinforce peacetime stability.[16] This would be a no-early-use, rather than a no-first-use, pledge. A no-early-use assurance, however, would require many of the steps sketched out in the preceding chapter to be taken to ensure command and control throughout a war, and to reassure the enemy that weapons were being held in reserve.

Another contentious but low-risk subject for diplomatic attention involves fissile-material production. Halting production would have little impact on current military capabilities. Pakistan's alleged suspension of HEU production has not changed Indian threat perceptions, and a bilateral freeze would not change those of Pakistan. Although India has resisted suspending production of fissile material, a bilateral cut-off would be symbolically valuable and would not diminish national security.

This issue is complicated in two ways, but a discussion group established at the June 1997 foreign secretary meetings may be able to overcome the problems. First, Pakistan is wary of a global fissile material cut-off convention (FMCC) because some analysts feel that the long hiatus in HEU production has put Islamabad at a strategic disadvantage.[17] Pakistan's unilateral constraint may have made a bilateral cut-off – even if India were prepared to discuss such an agreement – more difficult.[18] Resumed HEU production might cause India to accelerate its programme. At a minimum, resumption could reinforce India's conviction that Pakistan is not to be trusted. A further problem is India's continued reluctance to discuss restrictions until China and/or the global community makes more substantial progress towards nuclear disarmament. Since China, Russia and the US have ceased producing fissile material, an Indian freeze could be seen as part of a global pattern, rather than applying to India or South Asia alone. A freeze could also be enacted unilaterally and advertised as an example of the Gujral Doctrine in the nuclear field.

High Risk, Low Feasibility

Kashmir undoubtedly poses the most problems in bilateral relations. Although a discussion group was formed following the meetings in June, prospects for a stable solution are slim. It is vital, however, to take steps to reduce violence in Kashmir – on Pakistan's part, by cutting off support to insurgents, and on India's part, by withdrawing troops. Longer-term solutions, such as reviving UN resolutions and holding a plebiscite or recognising the Line of Control as the international boundary (which would require a change in India's Constitution), may be proposed at working-group level, but are unlikely to win much support, at least until deeper trust and confidence is established.[19] Although Kashmir poses high risks, it may be better to await improved relations on other fronts before tackling it.

The other major area of concern, but perhaps more to those outside South Asia, is nuclear proliferation. Proposed agreements to reduce the risks associated with nuclear confrontation have, however, little chance of success. George Perkovich of the Alton Jones Foundation proposed that both sides define and verify what level of proliferation would be allowed.[20] Facilities and components would be retained on both sides, but extensive inspection and monitoring arrangements, perhaps with third-party assistance, would need to be established. This would call for unprecedented monitoring provisions and is therefore unlikely. The agreement not to attack the other's nuclear facilities was relatively simple as it formalised the unstated awareness that neither side was planning a pre-emptive strike. Expanding that agreement to allow inspections of specified facilities has proved impossible. To meet the proposal that proliferation levels be verified would require monitoring nuclear facilities and components. This would call for a level of inspection well beyond what has already proved impossible to achieve.

Low Risk, Low Feasibility

Frequent proposals by the international non-proliferation community to declare or monitor the production or stockpiling of fissile material or to safeguard nuclear facilities would have little impact on security perceptions, but are politically sensitive and symbolically important. India and Pakistan resist being singled out in this area, and although Pakistan consistently proposes that inspection or monitoring agreements be reached, either through the International Atomic Energy Agency (IAEA) or third parties, they would do little to reduce threats. Focusing too much on these areas could also squander the opportunity to make progress on higher-risk issues. This is the case in other international regime-oriented approaches, such as one of Pakistan's standby offers, joint signing of the NPT. India perceives Pakistan's proposal for a five-party conference as an unnecessary external intrusion into South Asian politics.

Non-proliferation enthusiasts have also proposed a bilateral nuclear-test ban, which Pakistan has endorsed for years. A regional test ban would apparently affect neither basic nuclear research and development, nor the production of nuclear weapons. Islamabad has, by its own admission, achieved a nuclear capability without testing, while New Delhi has already conducted a test. A ban would probably constrain India and Pakistan from developing advanced weapons which would escalate the risks in a nuclear confrontation. Debate in India in 1996 over whether to test, and in India and Pakistan over how to respond to the CTBT, suggest that neither is likely to conduct a test.[21] Given its vociferous opposition to the CTBT, India is unlikely to agree to a regional test ban. Perhaps the best that can be hoped for is a long hiatus in nuclear testing by both sides that, in turn, could be formalised. Again, events on the ground suggest that further testing is unlikely, and emphasising this issue may deflect attention from more feasible and higher-risk concerns.

Conclusions

Diplomatic engagement is an important complement to unilateral security measures. Given that neither side can defend itself against nuclear attack, it is imperative that both continue to talk to each other. It would also help if China discussed nuclear-related CSBMs with India, but Chinese obduracy should not obscure the need for India and Pakistan to work bilaterally to reduce tensions and enhance stability.

A dialogue on missiles can establish political control over scientific developments that could seriously erode stability. Additional economic, military and nuclear disagreements can be addressed, but they do not pose the same threat as missile proliferation. A pair of high-risk issues, Kashmir and nuclear proliferation, may defy resolution until a habit of cooperation develops. A final set of ambitious but low-risk and unfeasible initiatives must await the outcome of negotiations about more volatile and contentious issues.

conclusion

For over 20 years, India and Pakistan have marched steadily towards nuclear proliferation. India began to focus on nuclear-weapon options after China's 1964 test; Pakistan did so eight years later. The pace has been measured as each has overcome obstacles thrown in their way by Western nations, as well as their own technical limitations. This limited technical progress has by now provided each with some basic nuclear capabilities which buttress the arguments for minimum deterrence. Ambiguity cloaks both programmes, allowing the two countries to limit arms competition and giving them the appearance of being non-proliferators, while allowing them to issue veiled nuclear threats.

This paper has argued that India and Pakistan's nuclear capabilities do not provide strategic stability. Furthermore, the introduction of ballistic missiles would strip away the ambiguity, put the countries on a hair-trigger footing and increase the likelihood that nuclear weapons will be used in a future war. The issue is no longer how to avoid nuclear proliferation, which may never have been in the interest of either country, but how to avoid nuclear use – which is presumably in the interest of both.

nuclear capabilities do not provide strategic stability

The simplest way to avoid nuclear use would be to reverse the nuclear programmes. This is unlikely in the short term as long as the world seems a dangerous place and India and Pakistan believe that nuclear weapons make it safer. Both agree that nuclear deterrence does so, while nuclear use does not. They thus face a dilemma confronted by other nuclear-armed states: how to make credible a threat which, if acted upon, could result in widespread destruction.

If India and Pakistan choose not to abandon nuclear weapons, but admit that war remains possible, it becomes necessary to assess how to fight a war either without using nuclear weapons or using them to minimal effect. Both countries have managed this problem by keeping their programmes underground, by acknowledging that they will not pre-empt, by arguing in favour of global or regional arms-elimination agreements and by refusing to be provoked by the other side. At the same time, they have developed their capabilities and increasingly become more public in their pronouncements. As Russia and the US have steadily reduced their nuclear stockpiles, as Argentina and Brazil have reversed their programmes, and as Belarus, Kazakstan, South Africa and Ukraine have eliminated their nuclear holdings, India and Pakistan increasingly stand out for their reluctance to consider these alternatives.

The introduction of ballistic missiles now threatens to accelerate this technical progress and increase the costs of conflict. Even if deployed, SRBMs would not constitute the bulk of India or Pakistan's nuclear-delivery means as aircraft will also be available. Nor will SRBMs be vulnerable once they are moved from their storage sheds. But just as Israel argued that it attacked Iraq's Osiraq reactor in 1981 to avoid a greater future threat, so too will there be a high premium during a crisis on neutralising delivery vehicles before they become threats, and on deploying them before they become targets. Both sides may feel pressed to assemble weapon components, load the missiles and move them from their storage sites early in a crisis. Demands on command and control will mount under such circumstances.

Sophisticated command-and-control measures may reduce ambiguity, thereby increasing the likelihood of war. However, this paper concludes that India and Pakistan's nuclear capabilities do not create stable deterrence because they are disconnected from the most probable precipitants of war. Without an adequate command-and-control system, the presence of nuclear weapons, regardless of whether they are assembled, increases the cost of war if deterrence fails. The addition of missiles to this unstable situation will shorten the fuse for decision-makers, increase tensions and reduce control during crises – but provide virtually no added security. In contrast, restricting missile development and deployment would sacrifice very little in security terms, while maintaining a time-delay during a crisis.

Waiting until a crisis occurs to think these issues through would reduce the number of decision-makers informing the debate, shorten the time available to reach a reasoned judgment and increase stress. It is clear that investing more resources on a bet that nuclear capabilities ensure safety only raises the penalties if the initial decision was wrong. Improved command and control and intensive diplomatic engagement would provide insurance that, if the bet is called, nuclear use is not the only choice.

Acknowledgements

The author would like to thank
Stephen Cohen, Melinda Erickson,
Frederick Mackie, Alden Mullins
and Ashley Tellis for their criticism
and comments. The author would
also like to thank George Perkovich
and the Alton Jones Foundation for
their financial support.

Introduction

[1] 'India Expresses Deep Concern
Over Pakistan's Missile Test',
'Pakistan Confirms Missile Test,
Says China Nuclear Link Within
Internationally Drawn Limits', *BBC
Summary of World Broadcasts (SWB)*,
Asia-Pacific, FE/2963, 5 July 1997,
p. A/1-A/3; 'India Moves Its New
Missile Near Pakistan', *International
Herald Tribune*, 4 June 1997, p. 6;
'India Denies Deployment of
Missiles', *International Herald
Tribune*, 5 June 1997, p. 4; 'Report
Cites China–Pakistan Missile
Links', *Washington Post*, 13 June
1996, p. A19; 'Irate State
Department Disputes Missile
Reports', *Associated Press*, 13 June
1996; 'China Denies Selling
Pakistan Nuclear-Capable M-11
Missiles', *Associated Press*, 13 June
1996; 'Pakistan Denies Deployment
of Chinese M-11 Missiles', *Agence
France Presse*, 13 June 1996.
[2] The debate over the utility of
nuclear weapons in South Asia is
by no means settled. See Brigadier
Vijai K. Nair, *Nuclear India* (New
Delhi: Lancer International, 1992);
P. R. Chari, *Indo-Pak Nuclear Stand-
off: The Role of the United States*
(New Delhi: Manohar Publishers,
1995); Abdul Sattar, 'Security and
Nuclear Stability in South Asia',
unpublished paper, February 1994;
Lieutenant-Colonel Babur Idris,
'Arms Race – The Case of India
and Pakistan', *The Citadel*, no. 2,
1995, pp. 55–80; K.
Subrahmanyam, 'Nuclear Force
Design and Minimum Deterrence
Strategy', in Bharat Karnad (ed.),
*Future Imperilled: India's Security in
the 1990s and Beyond* (New Delhi:
Viking, 1994), pp. 188–93; C. Raja
Mohan and Peter R. Lavoy,
'Avoiding Nuclear War', in Michael
Krepon and Amit Sevak (eds),

Crisis Prevention, Confidence Building and Reconciliation in South Asia (London: Macmillan Press, 1995), pp. 25–52; George Perkovich, 'A Nuclear Third Way in South Asia', *Foreign Policy*, no. 91, Summer 1993, pp. 85–104; Peter Lavoy, 'The Strategic Consequences of Nuclear Proliferation: A Review Essay', *Security Studies*, vol. 4, no. 4, Summer 1995; Devin T. Hagerty, 'Nuclear Deterrence in South Asia: The 1990 Indo-Pakistani Crisis', *International Security*, vol. 20, no. 3, Winter 1995–96, pp. 79–114; Gregory F. Giles and James E. Doyle, 'Indian and Pakistani Views on Nuclear Deterrence', *Comparative Strategy*, vol. 15, no. 2, April 1996, p. 146; Zia Mian (ed.), *Pakistan's Atomic Bomb and the Search for Security* (Lahore: Gautam Publishers, 1995).

[3] Their agreement not to attack one another's nuclear facilities, though unverifiable, provides at least superficial reinforcement of this conviction; see 'Pakistan and India Exchange Lists of Nuclear Installations', *SWB*, Asia-Pacific FE/2807, 3 January 1997, p. A/2. The text can be found in Sumit Ganguly and Ted Greenwood (eds), *Mending Fences: Confidence and Security Building Measures in South Asia* (Boulder, CO: Westview Press, 1997), Appendix One.

[4] Personal discussions with, among others, K. Subrahmanyam, New Delhi, April 1997, and General Nishat Ahmed, Islamabad, April 1997; Krishnaswami Sundarji, 'Changing Military Equations in Asia: The Relevance of Nuclear Weapons', in Francine R. Frankel (ed.), *Bridging the Non-proliferation Divide: The United States and India* (Lanham, MD: University Press of America, 1995), pp. 129–39; Niaz Naik, 'NPT Extension and its Implications for South Asia', *Strategic Perspectives*, vol. 3, no. 3, Summer 1995, p. 5.

[5] Of the 40,000 casualties suffered by the Indian Army since 1947, only 12,000 were the result of cross-border wars with Pakistan and China. Shekhar Gupta, *India Redefines its Role*, Adelphi Paper 293 (Oxford: Oxford University Press for the IISS, 1995), p. 25; Kotera M. Bhimaya, 'Nuclear Deterrence in South Asia', *Asian Survey*, vol. 34, no. 7, July 1994, pp. 655–56; Sandy Gordon, 'Resources and Instability in South Asia', *Survival*, vol. 35, no. 2, Summer 1993.

[6] Bharat Karnad, 'India's Weak Geopolitics and What To Do About It', in Karnad (ed.), *Future Imperilled*, pp. 16–84; Brigadier Vijai K. Nair, 'Nuclear Proliferation in South Asia: The Military Implications', *Indian Defence Review*, vol. 10, no. 1, January/March 1995, p. 27; P. R. Chari, *Managing Nuclear Proliferation in South Asia: An Indian View*, CISSM Papers 4 (College Park, MD: Center for International and Security Studies at Maryland, 1995), pp. 17–22; Gupta, *India Redefines its Role*, pp. 56–58. A dissenting view on whether China poses a threat can be found in Eric Arnett, 'What Threat?', *Bulletin of Atomic Scientists*, vol. 55, no. 2, March/April 1997, pp. 53–54.

[7] Neil Joeck, 'Nuclear Proliferation and Nuclear Reversal in South Asia', *Comparative Strategy*, vol. 16, no. 3, September 1997, pp. 263–73.

Chapter 1

[1] 'Pakistan Premier Calls for Removal of "Mistrust" in Relations

[speech by Prime Minister Nawaz Sharif]' and 'Indian Premier Outlines Priorities for Future Work of SAARC [Speech by Prime Minister Inder Gujral]', *SWB, Asia-Pacific*, FE/2919, 15 May 1997, pp. S2/8–10 and S2/16–20; 'Premier Gujral Optimistic about Strengthening Ties with Pakistan' and 'Pakistan Premier Calls Agreement with India "Major Breakthrough"', *SWB, Asia-Pacific*, FE/2954, 25 June 1997, p. A/2.

[2] The discussion of the 1987 *Brasstacks* crisis and the 1990 confrontation is based on numerous personal discussions and two important texts. The definitive study of *Brasstacks* is Kanti P. Bajpai, P. R. Chari, Pervaiz Iqbal Cheema, Stephen P. Cohen and Sumit Ganguly, *Brasstacks and Beyond: Perception and Management of Crisis in South Asia* (Urbana, IL: Program In Arms Control, Disarmament and International Security, University of Chicago at Urbana-Champaign, 1995). The most complete review of the 1990 confrontation is Michael Krepon and Mishi Faruqee, *Conflict Prevention and Confidence-Building Measures in South Asia: The 1990 Crisis*, Occasional Paper 17 (Washington DC: Henry L. Stimson Center, 1994). Other, less complete studies of the 1990 crisis can be found in Mitchell Reiss, *Bridled Ambition: Why Countries Constrain Their Nuclear Capabilities* (Washington DC: The Woodrow Wilson Center, 1995), pp. 189–92, and Hagerty, 'Nuclear Deterrence', pp. 91–112; Seymour Hersh's version of the 1987 and 1990 crises ('On the Nuclear Edge', *The New Yorker*, 23 March 1993, pp. 56–73) is unreliable and has been criticised by Hersh's own sources.

[3] Personal discussions, New Delhi and Islamabad, April 1997; Ashley J. Tellis, *Stability in South Asia*, RAND Documented Briefing (Santa Monica, CA: RAND Corporation, 1997), pp. 30–33; General Khalid Mahmud Arif, 'The Roots of Conflict in South Asia: A Pakistani Perspective', in Karnad (ed.), *Future Imperilled*, pp. 159–75; Subrahmanyam, 'Nuclear Force Design and Minimum Deterrence Strategy'; Vice-Admiral K. K. Nayar argued that India has no option other than to avoid a war with Pakistan in 'NPT Polemics: The South Asian Equation', *Indian Defence Review*, vol. 10, no. 1, January/March 1995, p. 18; Giles and Doyle, 'Indian and Pakistani Views', p. 146.

[4] C. Raja Mohan discusses crisis stability in 'Crisis Management and Confidence Building', in Frankel (ed.), *Bridging the Non-proliferation Divide*, pp. 181–203.

[5] Devin Hagerty (rapporteur), *Preventing Nuclear Proliferation in South Asia* (New York: The Asia Society, 1995), p. 17.

[6] An excellent overview of the recent history of the Kashmir issue can be found in Raju Thomas (ed.), *Perspectives on Kashmir: The Roots of Conflict in South Asia* (Boulder, CO: Westview Press, 1992); a brief update from early 1997 is available in Surinder Singh Oberoi, 'Kashmir is Bleeding', *Bulletin of the Atomic Scientists*, vol. 53, no. 2, March/April 1997, pp. 24–32; 'Indian Soldiers Kill 5 Rebels in Kashmir', *International Herald Tribune*, 13 June 1997, p. 5.

[7] 'Indian Prime Minister Interviewed on Domestic and Foreign Issues', *SWB, Asia-Pacific*, FE/2910, 5 May 1997, p. A/5; 'Pakistan Foreign Minister says

Kashmir Still a Core Issue', *SWB, Asia-Pacific*, FE/2924, 21 May 1997, p. A/4. Making clear that the June 1997 foreign-secretary meetings did not change this view, Indian Foreign Secretary Salman Haider emphasised that Kashmir was not disputed territory; Pakistani Prime Minister Nawaz Sharif asserted that improved ties would not come at the expense of Kashmir. See 'Kashmir not "Disputed Territory" in Talks with Pakistan', *SWB, Asia-Pacific*, FE/2956, 27 June 1997, p. A3; 'Pakistan Premier Notes Improving Ties with India, Not at Expense of Kashmir Cause', *SWB, Asia-Pacific*, FE/2963, 5 July 1997, p. A/3.

8 Before drawing conclusions about the events in Kashmir in 1947, it must be noted that, as Robert Wirsing writes, 'about these and other events ... there is nothing today even remotely resembling a consensus'. See *India, Pakistan, and the Kashmir Dispute* (London: Macmillan Press, 1994), p. 39; Pervaiz Iqbal Cheema, *Pakistan's Defence Policy, 1947–58* (London: Macmillan Press, 1990), pp. 85–93; Ayesha Jalal, *The State of Martial Rule: The Origins of Pakistan's Political Economy of Defence* (Cambridge: Cambridge University Press, 1990), p. 58; Sisir Gupta, *Kashmir: A Study in India–Pakistan Relations* (London: Asia Publishing House, 1966).

9 Cheema, *Pakistan's Defence Policy*, p. 87.

10 Edward Gargan, '12 Are Killed as Pakistani Police Fire on Kashmiris Marching Toward Border', *New York Times*, 13 February 1992, p. A-3.

11 Tellis, *Stability in South Asia*, pp. 47–48.

12 Bajpai *et al.*, *Brasstacks*, p. 21.

13 The best study of the war is Richard Sisson and Leo Rose, *War and Secession: Pakistan, India and the Creation of Bangladesh* (Berkeley, CA: University of California Press, 1979).

14 Sumit Ganguly, 'Ethno-Religious Conflict in South Asia', *Survival*, vol. 35, no. 2, Summer 1993; Raju Thomas, 'Managing Internal Security Problems', in Krepon and Sevak (eds), *Crisis Prevention*, pp. 107–30; K. P. S. Gill, 'The Dangers Within: Internal Security Threats', in Karnad (ed.), *Future Imperilled*, pp. 116–32.

15 Tellis notes that India's size and manipulation of its internal problems make internal disputes inherently controllable. See *Stability in South Asia*, pp. 40, 51ff.

16 Radio Pakistan reported that the MQM would be included in the cabinet. See *SWB, Asia-Pacific*, FE/2854, 27 February 1997, p. A/4; Susan Goldenberg, 'Power in Sight for Karachi's Disaffected', *The Guardian*, 1 February 1997, p. 9; 'Eight Killed in Karachi', *ibid.*, 19 January 1997, p. 16; 'President Meets MQM Party Delegates, Calls for Peace in Karachi', *SWB, Asia-Pacific*, FE/2956, 27 June 1997, p. A/3; 'Punjab CM hints at Banning Sectarian Parties', *The News* (Islamabad), 24 April 1997, p. 1; Pakistan's premature recognition of the *Taleban* as the government of Afghanistan in May 1997 underscores Islamabad's partisan views on the outcome of the war; see 'The Battle for Afghanistan', *The Economist*, 31 May 1997, pp. 67–68. It is interesting to note in this regard that little has changed in the past decade; see Mahnaz Ispahani, *Pakistan: Dimensions of Insecurity*, Adelphi Paper 246 (London: Brassey's for the IISS, 1989–90),

pp. 7–29.

[17] Personal discussions, New Delhi and Islamabad, April 1997; Tellis, *Stability in South Asia*, pp. 19–25; Hagerty, 'Nuclear Deterrence', pp. 82–91.

[18] Personal discussion with General Gul Hasan, March 1995; G. S. Bhargava, *India's Security in the 1980s*, Adelphi Paper 125 (London: IISS, 1976), p. 6.

[19] In the 1990 case, Prime Minister Benazir Bhutto refused to adjust her schedule to meet the US mediators. Unless forcible entry is threatened, therefore, third-party involvement is dependent on local decision-makers, who may refuse or prevent intervention. Personal discussions, Washington DC and Livermore, CA.

[20] Shirin Tahir-kheli, *The United States and Pakistan: The Evolution of an Influence Relationship* (New York: Praeger Publishers, 1982), pp. 33–43.

[21] General V. N. Sharma, 'India's Defence Forces: Building the Sinews of a Nation', *Journal of the United Service Institution of India*, vol. 124, no. 518, October/December 1994, pp. 449–50; Neville Maxwell, *India's China War* (London: Jonathan Cape, 1970), pp. 185–99; Richard Ned Lebow, *Between Peace and War: The Nature of International Crises* (Baltimore, MD: The Johns Hopkins Press, 1981), pp. 164–69; Stephen A. Hoffman, *India and the China Crisis* (Berkeley, CA: University of California Press, 1989).

[22] Gupta, *India Redefines its Role*, p. 34.

[23] Personal discussions with, among others, Inder Gujral, New Delhi, January 1984, and Los Angeles, 1985; Neil Joeck, *Nuclear Proliferation and National Security in India and Pakistan* (Ann Arbor, MI: University Microfilms, 1986), pp. 229ff.

[24] Personal discussion, New Delhi, April 1997; Krepon and Faruqee, *Conflict Prevention*, pp. 26–27.

[25] Robert Jervis, 'Introduction', in Jervis, Richard Ned Lebow and Janice Gross Stein (eds), *Psychology and Deterrence* (Baltimore, MD: The Johns Hopkins Press, 1985), p. 11.

Chapter 2

[1] This point, couched in terms of Indian cultural difference, was forcefully made by Colonel Sheketkhar in a seminar discussion at the Center for Policy Research, New Delhi, 14 April 1997.

[2] Basic introductions to the Indian and Pakistani nuclear programmes can be found in Ashok Kapur, *India's Nuclear Option* (New York: Praeger Publishers, 1976), and *Pakistan's Nuclear Dilemma* (New York: Plenum Publishers, 1987). Forthcoming books by Peter Lavoy, George Perkovich, W. P. S. Sidhu and Ashley Tellis provide detailed examinations of deterrence in South Asia.

[3] *Asian Recorder: Weekly Digest of Asian Events*, vol. 20, no. 23, 4–10 June 1974, pp. 12,033–34. Shastri was elliptical in his description of what would become the option policy: 'I cannot say that the present policy is deep-rooted … that it can never be changed … If there is need to amend what we have said, even we will say all right, let us go ahead and do so'.

[4] Lieutenant-General K. S. Sundarji (ed.), *Nuclear Weapons in Third World Context*, Combat Papers 2 (Mhow, India: College of Combat, August 1981) – hereafter referred

to as the *Mhow Papers*. Sundarji frequently expanded on the arguments of the *Mhow Papers*. See, for example, 'Changing Military Equations', in Frankel (ed.), *Bridging the Non-proliferation Divide*, and 'Imperatives of Indian Minimum Deterrence', *Agni: Studies in International Strategic Issues*, vol. 2, no. 1, May 1996, pp. 18–22; a brief dissent can be found in Bhimaya, 'Nuclear Deterrence', pp. 655–58.

[5] Steve Weissman and Herbert Krosney, *The Islamic Bomb: The Nuclear Threat to Israel and the Middle East* (New York: Times Books, 1981), chapters 4–6, 11–13.

[6] 'Khan Says India has Plutonium to make 50–70 Atom Bombs Anytime', *Nucleonics Week*, 20 June 1991, pp. 18–19; personal discussions in Islamabad, March 1995 and April 1997.

[7] Personal discussion with Dr Ishrat Usmani at the UN, New York, November 1983.

[8] Vice-Admiral K. K. Nayyar (Retd), 'NPT Polemics: The South Asian Equation', *Indian Defence Review*, vol. 10, no. 1, January/March 1995, pp. 17–20; personal discussion with Ambassador Maleeha Lodhi, who strongly rejected suggestions that Pakistan was insincere in its proposals, noting that they predated India's 1974 nuclear test (Islamabad, April 1997).

[9] Major-General Som Dutt, *India and the Bomb*, Adelphi Paper 30 (London: Institute for Strategic Studies, 1966).

[10] Sundarji in Sundarji (ed.), the *Mhow Papers*, pp. 18–19, 27–28.

[11] Vohra in *ibid.*, p. 40.

[12] Subrahmanyam in *ibid.*, p. 53.

[13] Dutt, *India and the Bomb*, p. 4.

[14] Sumit Ganguly, 'Indo-Pakistani Nuclear Issues and the Stability/ Instability Paradox', *Defence Today*, vol. 4, no. 2, April/June 1996, pp. 185–93; Tellis, *Stability in South Asia*, p. 32.

[15] Sundarji in Sundarji (ed.), the *Mhow Papers*, p. 19.

[16] *Ibid.*, pp. 19–20.

[17] General Mirza Aslam Beg, 'Pakistan's Nuclear Programme: A National Security Perspective', unpublished manuscript, p. 13.

[18] Dutt, *India and the Bomb*, p. 5.

[19] Pinto in Sundarji (ed.), the *Mhow Papers*, p. 11.

[20] Hasan-Askari Rizvi, *Pakistan's Nuclear Programme*, Pakistan Papers 2 (Karachi: Pakistan Association for Peace Research, 1991), p. 17.

[21] Sundarji, 'Changing Military Equations'; Subrahmanyam, 'Nuclear Force Design', pp. 185–95; Perkovich, 'A Nuclear Third Way'; Jasjit Singh, 'Prospects for Nuclear Proliferation', in Serge Sur (ed.), *Nuclear Deterrence: Problems and Perspectives in the 1990s* (New York: UN, 1993), pp. 66–67; and McGeorge Bundy, 'Existential Deterrence and its Consequences', in Douglas MacLean (ed.), *The Security Gamble: Deterrence Dilemmas in the Nuclear Age* (Totowa, NJ: Rowman and Allanheld, 1984), pp. 3–13.

[22] The concept of absolute security was developed by Bernard Brodie in *The Absolute Weapon* (Princeton, NJ: Princeton University Press, 1946).

[23] Personal discussion with Dr A. Q. Khan, Islamabad, April 1997.

[24] Tim Weiner, 'US Suspects India Prepares to Conduct Nuclear Test', *New York Times*, 15 December 1995, p. 1; John F. Burns, 'India Denies Atom-Test But Then Turns Ambiguous', *ibid.*, 16 December 1995, p. 8.

[25] Praful Bidwai, 'Battle for a Bona

Fide CTBT', *The Economic Times* (Mumbai), 1 April 1996, p. 7; Brahma Chellaney, 'Read All About It: India is Deploying Missiles', *International Herald Tribune*, 13 June 1997, p. 8.

[26] Suzanne Goldenberg, 'Pakistan N-test "Ready"', *The Guardian*, 7 March 1996, p. 3; Tom Rhodes, 'Pakistan Prepares Bomb Test', *The Times*, 7 March 1996, p. 3; 'Pakistan Said Ready to Counter Indian Nuclear Test with its Own', *Nucleonics Week*, 29 February 1996, p. 14; 'The Case for Going Nuclear', *The Muslim*, 25 February 1996, p. 1.

[27] Rahul Bedi, 'India Ignores West and Test Fires Prithvi II', *Jane's Defence Weekly*, 7 February 1996, p. 12; 'Foreign Minister warns of "Countermeasures" to Indian Missile Test', *SWB, Asia-Pacific*, EE/ D2528/A, 5 February 1996; Ahmed Rashid, 'Testing Times', *Far Eastern Economic Review*, 22 February 1996; 'India Moves Its New Missile Near Pakistan', *International Herald Tribune*, 4 June 1997, p. 6; Raja Ashgar, 'Pakistan Dismisses US, Indian Missile Fears', *Reuters*, 3 July 1997.

[28] Personal discussion with Dr Khan, Islamabad, April 1997.

[29] P. R. Chari, 'Defence Policy Formulation: The Indian Experience', *Indian Defence Review*, vol. 11, no. 1, January/March 1996, p. 32.

[30] Waldo Stumpf, 'South Africa's Nuclear Weapons Program: From Deterrence to Dismantlement', *Arms Control Today*, vol. 25, no, 10, December 1995/January 1996, pp. 3–8.

[31] Pakistan's General Beg made the same point, 'General Beg Claims Country Conducted "Cold" Nuclear Test', *Foreign Broadcast Information Service (FBIS)-NES*, 3 August 1993, p. 56; 'Test Not a Must to Prove Pak. N-Capabilities', *The Hindu*, 29 May 1989, p. 6.

[32] Sundarji, 'Changing Military Equations', p. 134; Mohan, 'Crisis Management', pp. 197–98.

[33] Sundarji, 'Changing Military Equations', pp. 132–33.

[34] Lieutenant-General J. F. R. Jacob (Retd), 'Towards Rationality in Defence Preparedness', *Journal of the United Service Institution of India*, vol. 125, no. 519, January/March 1995, p. 44.

[35] Sundarji, 'Changing Military Equations', pp. 134–36; Hagerty, 'Nuclear Deterrence', pp. 86–87. Target selection may also be governed by adverse weather conditions that could distribute fallout on one's own country, as well as by a reluctance to target certain ethnic groups (i.e., Indian Muslims, who tend to live in cities rather than in rural areas). See S. Rashid Naim, '*Aadhi Raat Ke Baad* (After Midnight)' in Stephen Philip Cohen (ed.), *Nuclear Proliferation in South Asia: The Prospects for Arms Control* (Boulder, CO: Westview Press, 1991), pp. 23–61; and Idris, 'Arms Race', pp. 77–78.

[36] 'Nuclear Ambivalence Versus a Well Defined Policy Involving Minimum Political Fallout', *The Citadel*, no. 2, 1994, p. 60.

[37] Raja Ramanna, 'Security, Deterrence, and the Future', *Journal of the United Service Institution of India*, vol. 122, no. 509, July/ September 1992, p. 287.

[38] Vohra in Sundarji (ed.), the *Mhow Papers*, p. 39; Subrahmanyam, 'Nuclear Deterrence', in Subrahmanyam (ed.), *India and the Nuclear Challenge* (New Delhi: Lancer International, 1986), p. 121.

[39] Vohra in Sundarji (ed.), the *Mhow*

Papers, p. 39.

[40] Sundarji, 'Changing Military Equations', p. 134.

[41] Subrahmanyam, 'The Indian Nuclear Test in a Global Perspective', *The Institute for Defence Studies and Analyses Journal*, vol. 7, no. 1, July/September 1974, p. 17.

[42] Chari in Sundarji (ed.), the *Mhow Papers*, p. 66.

[43] Vohra in *ibid.*, p. 39; Idris, 'Arms Race', p. 78.

[44] Sundarji argues in favour of component separation in 'Imperatives of Indian Minimum Nuclear Deterrence', *Agni: Studies in International Strategic Issues*, vol. 2, no. 1, May 1996, p. 17; component separation is implied by Perkovich, 'A Nuclear Third Way', pp. 85–91.

[45] 'Prospects for Nuclear Proliferation', in Sur (ed.), *Nuclear Deterrence*, pp. 66–67.

[46] Bhashyam Kasturi, 'Military Intelligence in India: An Analysis', *Indian Defence Review*, vol. 9, no. 1, January 1994, pp. 71–74; Lieutenant-General P. N. Kathpalia, 'Intelligence: Problems and Possible Solutions', *ibid.*, vol. 2, no. 1, January 1986, pp. 133–35; Ramanna, 'Security, Deterrence and the Future', p. 287; personal discussions, New Delhi, April 1997.

[47] Bruce Blair, 'Alerting in Crisis and Conventional War', in Ashton B. Carter, John D. Steinbruner and Charles A. Zraket (eds), *Managing Nuclear Operations* (Washington DC: The Brookings Institution, 1987), pp. 75–120.

[48] Chari, *Indo-Pak Nuclear Stand-off*, p. 219. Bhimaya argues that 'there is no evidence that India and Pakistan are heading toward a minimum deterrence posture'. See 'Nuclear Deterrence', p. 660.

[49] Personal discussions, New Delhi, April, 1997.

[50] Tellis, *Stability in South Asia*, pp. 19–25.

Chapter 3

[1] S. Hidayat Hasan, 'Command and Control of Nuclear Weapons in Pakistan', *Swords and Ploughshares*, vol. 9, no. 1, Autumn 1994, pp. 11–14; Brigadier G. B. Reddi, 'Defence Preparedness – Issues and Choices: An Agenda for the Twenty-First Century', *Indian Defence Review*, vol. 11, no. 2, April/June 1996, pp. 32–29; George K. Tanham, *Indian Strategic Thought: An Interpretive Essay* (Santa Monica, CA: RAND Corporation, 1992); Lieutenant-General K. K. Hazari, 'National Security: Future Threat and Challenges', *Agni: Studies in International Strategic Issues*, vol. 2, no. 1, May 1996, pp. 1–16 (on p. 10 he writes: 'one of India's major failings has been the lack of properly developed strategies to deal with various domestic and international issues that have impinged on her short and long term national security interests'); Brigadier Nair suggests that Pakistan may have a nuclear strategy in place in 'Nuclear Proliferation in South Asia', p. 27; Bhimaya, 'Nuclear Deterrence', pp. 649–58.

[2] Ashton B. Carter, John D. Steinbruner and Charles A. Zraket, 'Introduction', in Carter *et al.* (eds), *Managing Nuclear Operations*, p. 1.

[3] Munir Ahmed Khan, 'Containing Nuclear Arms Race in South Asia', unpublished background paper for Joint US–Pakistan Symposium, 1–2 June 1994, p. 11.

[4] *Ibid.*, p. 10.

[5] Prime Minister Bhutto said that Pakistan did not have a bomb 'constructed, assembled, ready to be used, and positioned on the table', FBIS/NESA, 20 July 1989, pp. 26–27; Foreign Secretary Shaharyar Khan stated that Pakistan had components which, if put together, would constitute a 'device' (*Washington Post*, 7 February 1992); Prime Minister Nawaz Sharif stated that Pakistan possessed an atom bomb (*India Today*, 15 September 1994, p. 47).

[6] Khan, 'Containing Nuclear Arms Race', p. 9.

[7] Subrahmanyam, 'It's Deterrence, Stupid', *Economic Times*, 19 June 1995, p. 7; 'US Missiles Target Third World', *The Sunday Times*, 9 February 1992, p. 1; Sundarji, 'Courting Disaster', *India Today*, 30 November 1991, p. 78.

[8] Stephen Peter Rosen, *Societies and Military Power: India and Its Armies* (Ithaca, NY: Cornell University Press, 1996), pp. 251–53.

[9] Nair, 'Nuclear Proliferation', p. 34; Sundarji's *Blind Men of Hindoostan: Indo-Pak Nuclear War* (New Delhi: UBS Publishers, 1993) is a thinly disguised lament about the exclusion of military commanders from Indian councils of war; personal discussions in New Delhi, April 1997.

[10] US practice is discussed by Donald R. Cotter, 'Peacetime Operations: Safety and Security', in Carter *et al.* (eds), *Managing Nuclear Operations*, pp. 24–30.

[11] Personal discussion with Air Commodore Jasjit Singh, New Delhi, April 1997.

[12] Cotter, 'Peacetime Operations', in Carter *et al.* (eds), *Managing Nuclear Operations*, pp. 42–50; in 'Security Implications of Nuclear Proliferation in South Asia', unpublished manuscript, 1994, p. 13, Munir Ahmed Khan argues that India and Pakistan 'do not appear to have a sound Control, Command and Communication System or enough know-how to install necessary safety measures which leave open the possibility of a nuclear mishap resulting in grave consequences'.

[13] Nayyar, 'Affordable Defence', in Karnad (ed.), *Future Imperilled*, pp. 152–53; Chari, *Indo-Pak Nuclear Stand-off*, pp. 185–94; Dr Swaran Singh, 'China's White Paper on Defence Policy', *Indian Defence Review*, vol. 11, no. 2, April/June 1996, pp. 29–31, argues that an Indian white paper would contribute to transparency; Nair, 'Nuclear Proliferation', pp. 27–34; personal discussions in New Delhi and Islamabad, April 1997.

[14] Lieutenant-General M. L. Thapar (Retd) notes that the military has not been integrated into nuclear planning in 'Musings on Defence', *Indian Defence Review*, vol. 11, no. 3, July/September 1996, pp. 32–33; John H. Sandrock, *Understanding India's Decision-making Process With Regard to Nuclear Weapons and Missile Development* (McLean, VA: Science Application International Corporation (SAIC), 15 December 1994), p. 24.

[15] Barry R. Posen, *The Sources of Military Doctrine* (Ithaca, NY: Cornell University Press, 1984), p. 13.

[16] Lieutenant-Colonel Syed Anwar Mehdi, 'Nuclear Ambivalence Versus a Well Defined Policy Involving Minimum Political Fallout', *The Citadel*, no. 2, 1994, pp. 55–61; more than a decade earlier, Major Farrakh Alam Shah argued that 'a limited nuclear war is a viable option and it can be

contained below the strategic threshold', see 'Nuclear Hardening of Equipment', *Pakistan Army Journal*, vol. 24, no. 1, Spring 1983, p. 3.

[17] Gupta, *India Redefines its Role*, pp. 38–39. This trend in defence spending is now being reversed; see 'India Plans Spending Hike', *Defense News*, vol. 12, no. 16, 21–27 April 1997, p. 8.

[18] Desmond Ball, 'Signals Intelligence (SIGINT) in Pakistan', *Strategic Analysis*, vol. 18, no. 2, May 1995, pp. 195–214.

[19] B. Raman, 'Intelligence Revamp: Some Aspects', *Journal of the United Service Institution of India*, vol. 126, no. 525, July/September 1996, pp. 300–16; Kasturi, 'Military Intelligence in India', pp. 71–74; Kathpalia, 'Intelligence: Problems and Possible Solutions', pp. 133–35.

[20] In 'Command and Control in Emerging Nuclear Nations', *International Security*, vol. 17, no. 3, Winter 1992–93, pp. 160–87, Peter D. Feaver details the assertive–delegative command structure distinction.

[21] Rosen, *Societies and Military Power*, p. 252.

[22] Colonel Kanwal Mago, 'Integration of the Ministry of Defence with Service Headquarters', *Journal of the United Service Institution of India*, vol. 126, no. 523, January/March 1996, pp. 42–55; Raman, 'National Security Management: Some Aspects', *ibid.*, vol. 125, no. 520, April/June 1995, pp. 164–75; Chari, 'Reforming the Ministry of Defence', *Indian Defence Review*, January 1991, pp. 46–53; Lieutenant-General Syed Refaqat (Retd), 'Twenty Years of Higher Defence Organization in Pakistan', *Pakistan Army Journal*, vol. 37, no. 3, Autumn 1996, pp. 3–10; K. K. Hazari and Vijai Nair, 'Higher Defence Planning: The Need for Debate and Reform', *Indian Defence Review*, vol. 8, no. 2, April 1993, pp. 33–40; Dipankar Banerjee, 'Consequences of Brass Tacks', *Journal of the United Service Institution of India*, vol. 135, no. 522, October/December 1995, pp. 535–38; Chari, *Managing Nuclear Proliferation*, p. 25.

[23] Air Commodore Singh argued that reserving a plane for post-nuclear attack delivery and getting it to its intended target would not be a significant problem (personal discussion, New Delhi, April, 1997).

[24] Ahmed Rashid, 'Fundamental Problem', *Far Eastern Economic Review*, 26 October 1995, p. 18. A powerful argument in favour of increasing the importance of Islam within the military was written by the general responsible for the aborted coup. See Major-General Zahir ul Islam Abbasi, 'The Quranic Concept of Leadership: Its Adoption and Application in the Pakistan Army', *The Citadel*, no. 1, 1992, pp. 35–51; a more cautious view appears in 'Army and Islam: An Appraisal', *Defence Journal* (Karachi), vol. 21, April/May 1996, pp. 3–9.

Chapter 4

[1] Michael Howard, 'Deterrence and Reassurance', *Foreign Affairs*, vol. 61, no. 2, Winter 1982–83, pp. 309–324; Subrahmanyam, 'Nuclear Deterrence', p. 111.

[2] Bajpai *et al.*, *Brasstacks*, pp. 13–24 and 59. A political tie between the foreign secretaries had also fallen into disuse and was only restored after the crisis; see 'Hotline Restored', *Dawn*, 28 April 1987,

p. 3.

[3] See various articles on CTBT in *Agni: Studies in International Strategic Issues*, vol. 2, no. 2, September/December 1996; Savita Datt, 'A Comprehensive Test Ban – Problems and Prospects', *Indian Defence Review*, vol. 10, no. 1, January/March 1995, pp. 21–26; G. Balachandran, 'CTBT and India', *Strategic Analysis*, vol. 19, no. 3, June 1996, pp. 493–506; a more positive view is contained in T. T. Poulose, *The CTBT and the Rise of Nuclear Nationalism in India* (New Delhi: Lancers Books, 1996).

[4] Ispahani, *Pakistan: Dimensions of Insecurity*, p. 36; Stephen Philip Cohen, 'Policy Implications', in Cohen (ed.), *Nuclear Proliferation*, pp. 359–66; Sundeep Waslekar, *Indian and Pakistani Approaches Towards Nuclear Non-proliferation*, Programme for Strategic and International Security Studies (PSIS) Occasional Paper No. 1 (Geneva: Graduate Institute of International Studies, 1993). A useful discussion of the problems inherent in CSBMs can be found in Marie-France Desjardins, *Rethinking Confidence-Building Measures*, Adelphi Paper 307 (Oxford: Oxford University Press for the IISS, 1997).

[5] The need for an institutionalised dialogue is frequently noted. See, for example, Nazir Kamal, 'The Future of Nuclear Weapons: Proliferation in South Asia', in Patrick J. Garrity and Steven A. Maaranen (eds), *Nuclear Weapons in the Changing World* (New York: Plenum Press, 1992), p. 191; and Mani Shankar Aiyar, 'Four Options', *Peace Initiatives*, vol. 1, no. 1, July/August 1995, p. 50; Ahmed Khan, 'Nuclear Arms Race', p. 21.

[6] Rahul Bedi, 'India Urged to take Agni to its "Logical Conclusion"', *Jane's Defence Weekly*, vol. 27, no. 18, 7 May 1997, p. 5; '"Remarkable Progress" in Guided Missile Programme During 1996–97 Reported', *SWB*, FE/2893, 15 April 1997, p. A/2; 'India Completes Research on Nuclear Missile', *Financial Times*, 6 December 1996, p. 1; R. Jeffrey Smith, 'China Linked to Pakistani Missile Plant', *Washington Post*, 25 August 1996; Tim Weiner, 'US Suspects China Is Giving Pakistan Help With Missiles', *New York Times*, 26 August 1996, p. A4; Fahmida Ashraf, 'India: A Missile Power', *Strategic Perspectives*, vol. 2, no. 3, Summer 1994, pp. 39–47.

[7] It is not surprising that the Indian military has shown relatively little enthusiasm for the *Prithvi*. For background on its development, see Pravin Sawhney, 'Prithvi's Position: India Defends its Missile', *Jane's International Defence Review*, vol. 30, July 1997, pp. 43–45; Wing Commander J. P. Joshi (Retd), 'Employment of Prithvi Missiles', *Journal of the United Service Institution of India*, vol. 126, no. 526, October/December 1996, pp. 463–70; Raj Chengappa, 'Boosting the Arsenal', *India Today*, 29 February 1996, pp. 98–99; Sundeep Waslekar, *Abolishing Nuclear Weapons: Rajiv Gandhi Plan Revisited*, ACDIS Occasional Paper (Urbana, IL: Program in Arms Control, Disarmament, and International Security, University of Illinois at Urbana-Champaign, July 1994), p. 9.

[8] Personal discussions, Islamabad, April 1997.

[9] Chari, *Managing Nuclear Proliferation*, p. 19; although Indians frequently refer to Chinese missiles based in Tibet, Chinese officials

deny their presence.

[10] Personal discussion, Islamabad, June 1993; Ravi Rikhye and Pushpindar Singh discuss the M-11's threat in 'External Threats and India's Conventional Capabilities: Perspectives Till 2010', in Karnad (ed.), *Future Imperilled*, p. 102.

[11] Karnad stresses the utility of military-to-military CSBMs in 'Key to Confidence Building in South Asia: Fostering Military-to-Military Links', *Journal of the United Service Institution of India*, vol. 126, no. 524, April/June 1996, pp. 168–96.

[12] Sumit Ganguly, *Slouching Towards a Settlement: Sino-Indian Relations 1962–1993*, Occasional Paper 60 (Washington DC: Woodrow Wilson Center, 1994); Hazari, 'National Security', pp. 5–6; Zhao Weiwen and Giri Deshingkar, 'Improving Sino-Indian Relations', and Kanti Bajpai and Bonnie L. Coe, 'Confidence Building Between India and China', both in Krepon and Sevak (eds.), *Crisis Prevention*, pp. 227–38 and 199–226.

[13] Inder Gujral, 'Security Concerns in Asia in the Early 21st Century', *Journal of the United Service Institution of India*, vol. 126, no. 527, January/March 1997, pp. 2–7.

[14] 'India to Purchase Surplus Power from Pakistan', *SWB, Asia-Pacific*, FEW/0487, 21 May 1997, p. WA/1;

'Premier says No "Excess" Electricity Available for India', *SWB, Asia-Pacific*, FE 2925, 22 May 1997, p. A/4.

[15] Ispahani, *Pakistan: Dimensions of Insecurity*, p. 34.

[16] Mohan, 'Crisis Management', in Ganguly and Greenwood (eds), *Mending Fences*, pp. 197–98.

[17] Major Ihsan-Ul-Haq Khalid, 'India's Intended Second Nuclear Test – Implications', *Pakistan Army Journal*, vol. 37, no. 2, Summer 1996, pp. 43–46.

[18] 'Prime Minister says Country will not Yield to Foreign Pressure on Nuclear Option', *SWB, Asia-Pacific*, FE/2934, 2 June 1997, p. A/6.

[19] Turning the Line of Control into the international border is discussed in Nayyar, 'The Pakistani Challenge: Reality or Myth?', *Indian Defence Review*, vol. 8, no. 2, April 1993, p. 14; other approaches can be found in Gupta, *India Redefines its Role*, pp. 30–31.

[20] Perkovich, 'Nuclear Third Way', pp. 98–99.

[21] Brahma Chellaney, 'India Must No Longer Ignore its Nuclear Imperatives', *The Pioneer*, 17 January 1996, p. 8; G. Balachandran, 'Keeping the Option Open: India's Nuclear Dilemma', *Strategic Analysis*, vol. 18, no. 12, March 1996, pp. 1,579–88.